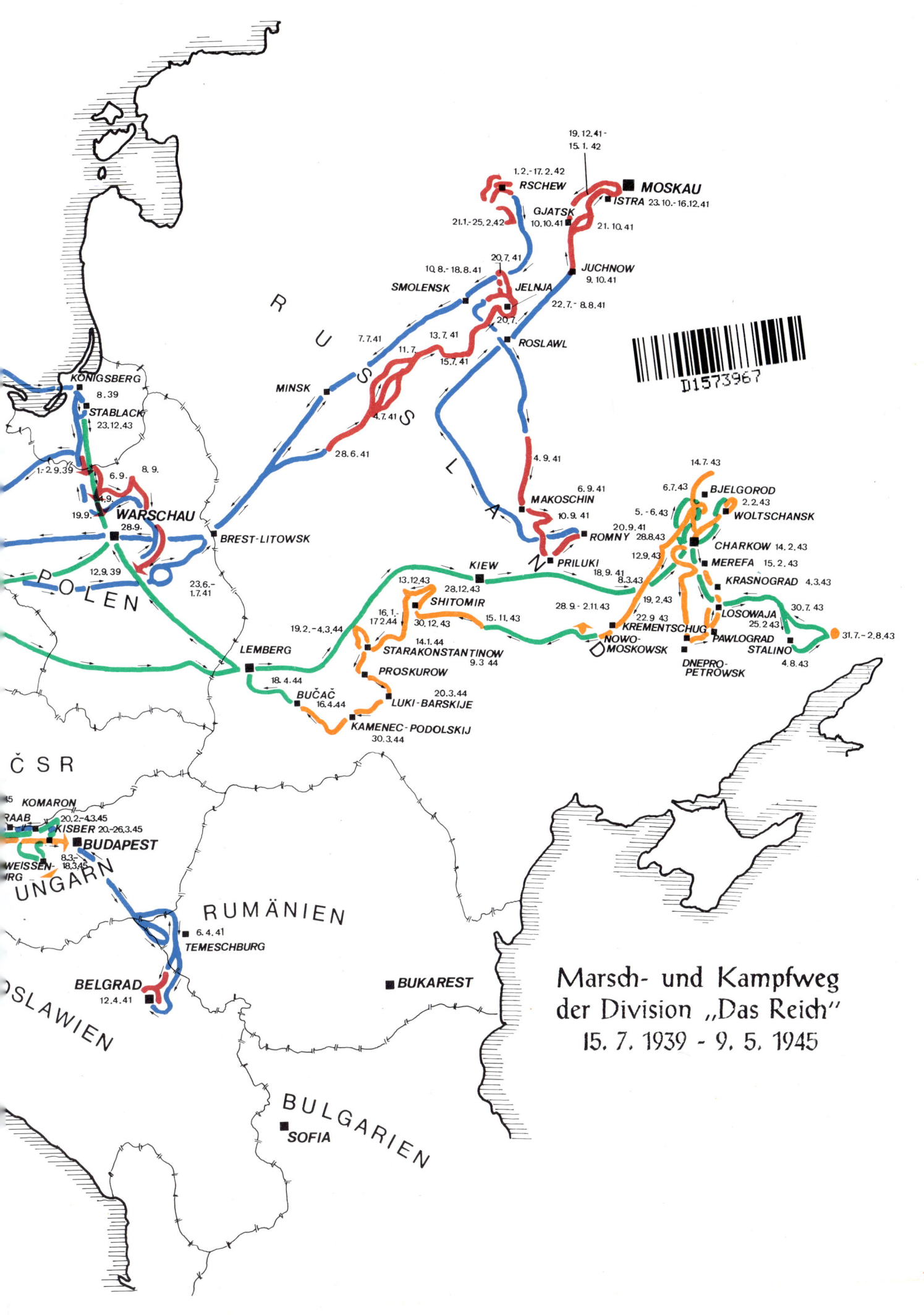

Otto Weidinger · Division Das Reich im Bild

OTTO WEIDINGER

DIVISION DAS REICH IM BILD

MUNIN-VERLAG GMBH, OSNABRÜCK

3. Auflage 1987

Copyright 1981 MUNIN-Verlag GmbH, D 4500 Osnabrück

Gestaltung und Herstellung Helmut Thöle

Karten Heinz Lindner

Schutzumschlag Ingeborg Clemens

Bildbeigaben aus Privatbesitz: Ernst Barkmann, Ferry Fendt, Heinz Harmel, Karl Kreutz, Otto Kumm, Heinz Macher, Walter Schallowetz, Gerd Schmager, Heinz Stutterecker, Helmut Thöle, Otto Weidinger und G.E. Wisliceny

Bilder aus den Archiven: Bundesarchiv, Munin-Verlag, Stalling-Verlag, Editions Heimdal, Archiv W. Ott und der Regimentskameradschaft „DF".

Soweit festgestellt werden konnte, sind die folgenden ehem. Kriegsberichter, insbesondere vom 1. Zug der 2. Kompanie („Kurt Eggers") mit Fotografien vertreten: Peter Adendorf, Kurt Albert, Ferdinand Fritsch, Hermann Grönert, Walter Lex, Willi Merz, Peter Neumann, Werner Zeymer, Friedrich Zschäckel.

ISBN 3-921242-45-2

Copyright 1981 by MUNIN-Verlag GmbH, D 4500 Osnabrück

Arrangement and production Helmut Thöle

Maps Heinz Lindner

Dust-cover Ingeborg Clemens

Photographs supplemented from personal property: Ernst Barkmann, Ferry Fendt, Heinz Harmel, Karl Kreutz, Otto Kumm, Heinz Macher, Walter Schallowetz, Gert Schmager, Heinz Stutterecker, Helmut Thöle, Otto Weidinger and G.E. Wisliceny

Photographs from archives: Bundesarchiv, MUNIN-Verlag, Stalling-Verlag, Editions Heimdal, Archiv W. Ott und Regimental Association „DF".

As far as could be identified the following war-correspondents are represented by photographs — above all those of 1 Platoon, 2 Company („Kurt Eggers") —: Peter Adendorf, Kurt Albert, Ferdinand Fritsch, Hermann Grönert, Walter Lex, Willi Merz, Peter Neumann, Werner Zeymer, Friedrich Zschäckel.

ISBN 3-921242-45-2

*Der preussische Gehorsam
ist der
einer freien Entscheidung,
nicht der
einer unterwürfigen Dienstwilligkeit*

„The Prussian obedience is that one of a free decision,
not that one of a submissive docility."

*In Verehrung unserem Erzieher und Lehrer gewidmet,
dem Senior der ehemaligen Soldaten der Waffen-SS
Paul Hausser
SS-Oberstgruppenführer und Generaloberst der Waffen-SS
zuletzt
Oberbefehlshaber der Heeresgruppe „G"
Träger des Ritterkreuzes
mit Eichenlaub und Schwertern*

Dedicated in devoted admiration to our educator and instructor,
the Senior of the former soldiers of the Waffen-SS
Paul Hausser
SS-Oberstgruppenführer and Colonel-General of the Waffen-SS.
In the end of the war Commander-in-Chief of Army-Group „G",
decorated with the Knights Cross-Oakleaves
and Swords.

Generalkommando
XXXXVI. Pz. Korps   Korps-Gef.-St., den 10.8.1941

Korps-Tagesbefehl Nr. 5

Nach einem der schweren Abwehrkämpfe an der Nordost-Front von Jelnja wurde die Gruppe Förster der 1./SS-Kradschützen-Bataillon, die den Auftrag hatte, die linke Flanke der Kompanie zu sichern, wie folgt aufgefunden:

> *Der Gruppenführer, SS-Unterscharführer Förster, mit der Hand an der Abreißschnur der letzten Handgranate, Kopfschuß.*
> *Schütze 1, SS-Rottenführer Klaiber, das MG noch in die Schulter eingezogen und ein Schuß im Lauf, Kopfschuß.*
> *Schütze 2, SS Sturmmann Buschner,*
> *Schütze 3, SS-Sturmmann Schyma, tot in den Schützenlöchern.*
> *Der Solomelder, SS-Sturmmann Oldeboerhuis, tot an der Maschine kniend mit der Hand am Lenker, gefallen in dem Augenblick, als er die letzte Meldung überbringen sollte.*
> *Der Fahrer, SS-Sturmmann Schwenk, tot in seinem Schützenloch.*

Vom Gegner sah man nur noch Tote, die auf Handgranatenwurfweite im Halbkreis um die Stellung der Gruppen lagen.
Ein Beispiel für den Begriff „Verteidigung"! In Ehrfurcht stehen wir vor solchem Heldentum!
Ich habe beantragt, daß diese Namen im Ehrenblatt des deutschen Heeres veröffentlicht werden.

Verteiler: Der Kommandierende General
(bis Komp.)   gez. v. Vietinghoff
                                              General der Panzertruppen

Das waren die Männer der 2. SS-Panzerdivision „Das Reich", die vom ersten bis zum letzten Kriegstag an fast allen Fronten gekämpft haben, von einem Brennpunkt zum anderen gehetzt, erfüllt von glühender Liebe zu Volk und Vaterland, von dem unbedingten Bewußtsein ihrer Pflicht, viele tausende mit dem Opfer ihres jungen Lebens.

Von ihnen berichtet dieses Buch.

Legende
der 2. SS-Panzerdivision „Das Reich"

Stammeinheiten (SS-Verfügungstruppe) 1933-35 aufgestellt:
Regiment „Deutschland" in München und Ellwangen,
Regiment „Germania" in Hamburg, Arolsen und Wolterdingen,
     später Radolfszell,
Pionier-Bataillon in Dresden-Leisnig,
Nachrichten-Abteilung in Adlershof, später Unna.

1938 aufgestellt:
Regiment „Der Führer" in Wien, Graz und Klagenfurt,
Aufklärungs-Abteilung in Ellwangen,
Kradschützen-Bataillon in Ellwangen,
Artillerie-Regiment in Jüterbog.

Nach dem Polenfeldzug Zusammenfassung dieser Einheiten zur SS-V-Division.

Bezeichnungen:

10.X.39-1.IV.40	SS-VT.-Division (mot)
1.IV.40-1.XII.40	SS-V.-Division
1.XII.40-21.XII.40	SS-Division „Deutschland"
21. XII.40-V.42	SS-Division „Reich"
V.42-9.XI.42	SS-Division „Das Reich"
9.XI.42-I.44	SS-Panzergrenadier Division „Das Reich"
I.44-V.45	2. SS-Panzer-Division „Das Reich"

General Command
XXXXVI Panzer Corps

Corps Battle H.Q. 10.8.1941

Corps Orders of the Day No. 5

After one of hard defensive battles on the north-east front of Jelnja, Förster's Group of the 1st Motorcycle Battalion which was assigned to cover the left flank of the company, was found as follows:

The group leader, SS Unterscharführer Förster, with his hand on the release cord of his last grenade, was shot in the head.

Rifleman No. 1, SS-Rottenführer Klaiber, his M-G still at his shoulder and a cartridge in the breech, was shot in the head.

Rifleman No. 2, SS Sturmmann Buschner,

Rifleman No. 3, SS-Sturmmann Schyma, dead in foxholes.

The dispatch rider, SS-Sturmmann Oldeboerhuis, was dead on his knees by his motorcychle, with his hands on the handlebars, killed in that moment as he sought to deliver the last dispatch.

The driver, SS-Sturmmann Schwenk, was dead in his foxhole.

Of the enemy, here were only dead men to be seen who lay in a semicircle around the group's position, a hand grenade's throwing distance away.

An example of what „Defence" means! We stand in respect and awe before such heroism!

I have applied for these names to be published in the Roll of Honour of the German Army.

General Officer Commanding
signed von Vietinghoff-Scheel
General of the Panzer Troops

These were the men of 2nd SS Panzer Division „Das Reich" who fought from the first to the last day of the war on almost every front, who rushed from one battle crisis to another, filled with a burning love of their people and fatherland, with absolute consciousness of their duty, many thousands of them sacrificing their young lives.

This book tells of them.

Roll-Call
of the 2nd SS Panzer Division „Das Reich"

Original unit (SS Verfügungstruppe) formed 1933-35:
Regiment „Deutschland" in Munich and Ellwangen,
Regiment „Germania" in Hamburg, Arolsen und Wolterdingen,
    later Radolfszell,
Pioneer-Battalion in Dresden-Leisnig,
Signals Battalion in Adlershof, later Unna.
Formed 1938:
Regiment „Der Führer" in Vienna, Graz and Klagenfurt,
Reconnaissance Battalion in Ellwangen,
Motorcycle Battalion in Ellwangen,
Artillery-Regiment in Jüterbog.
After the Polish Campaign, these units were reformed into the SS V-Division.

Titles:

10.X.39-1.IV.40	SS VT-Division (motorized)
1.IV.40-1.XII.40	SS V-Division
1.XII.40-21.XII.40	SS Division „Deutschland"
21. XII.40-V.42	SS Division „Reich"
V.42-9.XI.42	SS Division „Das Reich"
9.XI.42-I.44	SS Panzer Grenadier-Division „Das Reich"
I.44-V.45	2nd SS Panzer Division „Das Reich"

Vereidigung der SS-Verfügungstruppe am 8.11.35 vor der Feldherrenhalle.
The SS Verfügungstruppe takes the oath on 8.11.35 in front of the Feldherrnhalle.

So lange Mut und und Treue Werte bleiben, soll ihr Gedächtnis edel sein.
As long as courage and loyalty are esteemed, they will be held in noble memory.

Paul Hausser, Kommandeur der SS-Junkerschule Braunschweig,
der spätere Inspekteur, und Mathias Kleinheisterkamp, Taktiklehrer (1935),
beide aus der Reichswehr, wiesen der noch jungen Truppe den Weg.

Paul Hausser, commander and later inspector of the SS Junker school in Brunswick,
and Mathias Kleinheisterkamp, tactical instructor (1935),
both from the Reichswehr, they showed the way to the still youthful troop.

Appell des II. Bataillons des Infanterie-Regimentes „Germania".

II Battalion of the Infantry Regiment „Germania" on parade.

Signal zum Einsteigen.
Truppenübungsplatz Königsbrück

The signal to get on.
Königsbrück military training area.

Sportausbildung II./„Germania".

Sports training II „Germania".

Beseler-Steg.
Letzter Bock wird gesetzt.
Truppenübungsplatz Sennelager
Oktober 1935

Besel military bridge.
The last support is positioned.
Sennelager training area, October 1935.

3. Zug 1. Komp. Regt. „Germania" auf dem Marsch in die Lüneburger Heide.

3rd Platoon of the 1st Company, Regiment „Germania" marching in Lüneburg Heath.

Wachzug des I./SS („Deutschland") bei den Festspielen in Bayreuth unter Karl Ullrich.

The guard detachment of I SS („Deutschland") at the Bayreuth Festival, led by Karl Ullrich.

Czech
Harmel
Kraas
Tappe
Phiel
am 9.11.35 in München (1. Kp./Rgt. „Germania").

Czech
Harmel
Kraas
Tappe
Phiel
on 9.11.35 in Munich (1st Company, Regiment „Germania").

Die Nachrichten-Staffel der 8. Kompanie des Regiments „Deutschland" München.

The signals staff of the 8th Company of the Regiment „Deutschland" in Munich.

Das Regiment „G" verlädt zum Truppenübungsplatz Altengrabow (1935).

The Regiment „Germania" prepares to go to the Altengrabow military training area (1935).

8. Kompanie (MGK) „Deutschland" beim Gefechtsschießen mit schweren Maschinengewehren.

The 8th Company (motorcycle-machine gun) „Deutschland" — firing practice with heavy machine guns.

„Am siebten Tag schuf Gott im Zorn das Sennelager bei Paderborn".

„God in anger on the seventh morn, Created Sennelager camp at Paderborn."

Paul Hausser
SS-Oberführer und Kommandeur der Junkerschule Braunschweig 1935 auf dem Truppenübungsplatz Senne bei Paderborn.

Paul Hausser
SS Oberführer and commander of the Junker (officer training) School Brunswick in 1935, at the Senne training area near Paderborn.

Junkerschüler kehren 1935 von einer Gefechtsübung zur Junkerschule Braunschweig zurück.

Junker return from a battle exercise to the Junker School, Brunswick in 1935.

Vorbeimarsch der 2. Kompanie des SS-Regiments „Deutschland" 1936 vor SS-Obersturmbannführer Keppler. Kp.Chef SS-Hauptsturmführer Bittrich, Regimentsmusikzug unter SS-Hauptsturmführer Bunge.

The 2nd Company of the SS Regiment „Deutschland" marches past SS Obersturmbannführer Keppler 1936. Company commander SS Hauptsturmführer Bittrich, regimental bandsmen under SS Hauptsturmführer Bunge.

Spindinhalt in tadelloser Ordnung

Locker contents in immaculate order

Die Maschinengewehrkompanie des II. Batl. „Deutschland" (8./SS-„D")

The machine gun company of the II Battalion „Deutschland" (8th SS „Deutschland").

Parade der Regimenter der SS-Verfügungstruppe. Besuch Mussolini 1936 (München).

Parade of the SS-Verfügungstruppe regiments. Mussolini's visit, Munich 1936.

1. Kp. „Deutschland".

1st Company „Deutschland".

Rückmarsch von der Trauerparade für E. Peters. 12. Kp. (MGK) „Germania" Wolterdingen.

Marching back from the funeral parade for E. Peters. 12th (motorcycle-machine gun) Company „Germania" Wolterdingen.

10. Kp. „Germania" 8.10.36 auf dem Marsch zum Truppenübungsplatz Bergen in Soltau.

10th Company „Germania" marching to the training area Bergen in Soltau, 8.10.36.

Ausflug zur Zugspitze Gruppe Franz Höfer, SS-Rottenführer des SS-Rgt. „Deutschland".

SS Rottenführer of the SS Regiment „Deutschland", Franz Höfer's group excursion to the Zugspitze.

Und ständig zur Gefechtsausbildung zum Truppenübungsplatz. (Hier „Germania" im Sennelager)

They went constantly to the military training areas for battle training. (Here „Germania" at Sennelager)

Eine Goldmedaille bei der Geländefahrt im Harz 1936 für Mühlenkamp und seine Kradschützen; kommandiert zum Kradschützenbataillon 2 des Heeres (2. Pz.-Div. Eisenach).

Mühlenkamp and his motorcycle infantry get a gold medal for their cross-country drive. He was seconded to the 2nd Battalion of the Army (Heer) (2nd Panzer Div. Eisenach).

Schieß-Ausbildung am schweren Maschinengewehr (wassergekühltem MG 08) auf den Truppenübungsplatz Altengrabow.

Firing practice with heavy machine guns (water-cooled MG 08) at the Altengrabow training area.

Die Brückenkolonne des SS-Pionierbataillons — Übung außerhalb Dresdens.

The bridging column of the SS Pioneer Battalion — an exercise outside Dresden.

Die Pioniere bei Sport und Spiel.

The pioneers at sport and leisure.

Abschied der SS-Pioniere vom Truppenübungsplatz Altengrabow, der mit den unter Soldaten üblichen Gebräuchen den Nachfolgern überlassen wurde.

Departure of the SS pioneers from the Altengrabow training area which is handed over to their successors with the customary formalities among soldiers.

Die Patenschaft des Panzerschiffes „Deutschland" zum gleichnamigen Regiment der SS-Verfügungstruppe

The armoured ship „Deutschland" adopted the SS Verfügungstruppe regiment of the same name

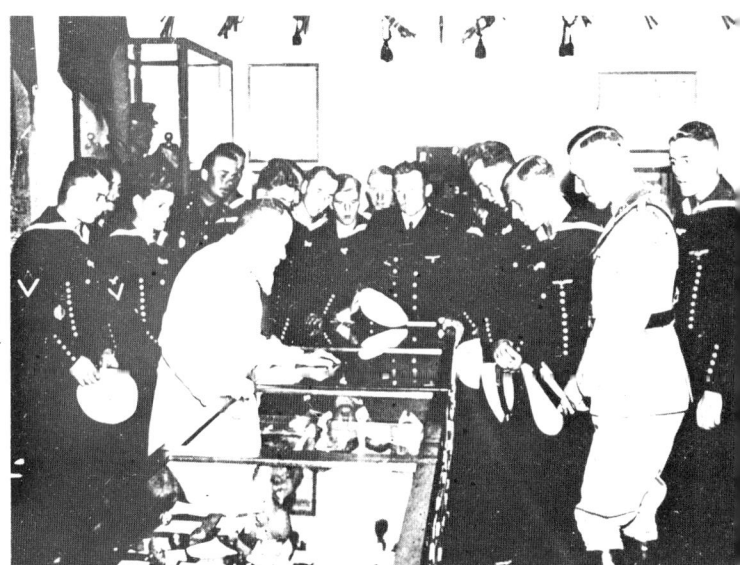

führte zu gegenseitigen Besuchen. Hier sind die Männer des Schiffes Gäste des Regimentes in München (Verwundete von „Ibiza"-Flugzeugangriff der Rotspanier auf das Schiff).

and this led to reciprocal visits. Here men of the ship's crew are the guests of the regiment in Munich (casualties from the „Ibiza" air attack on the ship by the Spanish communists).

1. Komp. „Deutschland" beim Probevorbeimarsch. SS-Obersturmführer Baldur Keller.
1. Zugf. Rohde (gefallen).

1st Company „Deutschland" during a practice march past. SS Obersturmführer Baldur Keller.
1st Platoon leader Rohde (killed in action).

Funkwagen mit Besatzung.

Radio vehicle with crew.

Apfelschimmel „Nikolaus" vom Trompeterkorps der Nachrichten-Abteilung unter SS-Oberscharführer Meier.

The dappled grey „Nikolaus" of the Signals Battalion trumpet corps under SS Oberscharführer Meier.

Die neue Kaserne in Unna, Block 2 und 3.

The new barracks in Unna, Block 2 and 3.

24 Männer der Nachrichten-Abteilung auf der Spree bei einer Kahnfahrt, als ihr Standort in Berlin-Adlershof lag.

24 men of the Signals Battalion in a boat on the Spree, at the time they were stationed in Berlin-Adlershof.

3,7 cm Panzerabwehrkanone in Stellung.

3.7 cm anti-tank gun in position.

Manöverkritik durch einen General des Heeres. In der Bildmitte SS-Standartenführer Keppler und SS-Sturmbannführer Bittrich.

A general of the Army (Heer) reviews manoevres. In the middle of the picture, SS Standartenführer Keppler and SS Sturmbannführer Bittrich.

Gepäckmarschmannschaft des IV./„Deutschland" unter Otto Weidinger zweitbeste bei den Meisterschaften in Hamburg 1938.

The pack march team of IV „Deutschland" under Otto Weidinger came second in the championship in Hamburg 198.

Ein Erinnerungsfoto der 8. Maschinengewehr-Kompanie des II. Bataillons SS-Standarte „Germania".

A photograph recalling the 8th machine gun company of II Battalion Standarte „Germania".

Sonnenwendfeier
beim Regiment „Deutschland".

Regiment „Deutschland"
at the midsummernight celebrations.

Paradeaufstellung II./„Germania" auf dem Kasernenhof des soldatenfreundlichen Städtchens Arolsen.

II „Germania" parading on the barracks square in the little town of Arolsen where the soldiers were popular.

Kasernentor SS-Pionier-Bataillon Dresden Hellerhof-Kaserne für 682 Soldaten mitten im Wald.

Barrack gates of the SS Pioneer Battalion in Dresden Hellerhof-quarters for 682 soldiers in the middle of woods.

Kriegsbrückengerät über die Pleisse eingesetzt.

A prefabricated military bridge is installed across the river Pleisse.

3./SS-Pi.Btl. beim Gesteinsbohren.

3rd Company Engineers Battalion drilling holes in rock.

Die schöne Garnison der SS-Pioniere war Dresden an der Elbe.

The beautiful garrison of the SS Pioneers war Dresden on the Elbe.

Aufmarsch zur Feld-Parade s. MG-Begleitzug vierspännig vom Sattel.

Forming up the heavy machine gun field parade — four-in-hand leading the escort company.

Truppenübungsplatz Altengrabow. Kriegsnahe Gefechtsausbildung.

Altengrabow training area. Realistic combat training.

Truppe im Biwak.
A unit in bivouac.

Die ersten Einberufungen zu III. Bataillon „Germania".

The first recruitments to III Battalion „Germania".

SS-Sturmbannführer Köppen (gefallen) kommandierte III./SS-„Germania".

SS Sturmbannführer Köppen (killed in action) commanded III SS „Germania".

Es gab viele Militär-Hornsignale.

Ther were many military bugle calls.

Vorbeimarsch des Regimentes „Germania" — hier schwenken der Spielmannszug und der Musikzug vor dem Hamburger Rathaus ein.

March past by the Regiment „Germania" — here the drum and fife musicians and the regimental bandsmen wheel round the town hall of Hamburg.

Parade vor Admiral Horthy August 1938. SS-Hauptsturmführer Ax führt 2./SS-„N".

Parading before Admiral Horthy August 1938. SS Hauptsturmführer Ax leads the 2nd SS „N".

SS-Sturmbannführer Buch, Kommandeur Nachrichten-Abteilung, verabschiedet sich.

SS Sturmbannführer Buch, commander of the Signals Battalion takes his leave.

Hier von den Jüngsten der Kompanien

Here from the youngest of the companies

und von der Fernsprechkompanie.

and from the telephone communications company.

Motorsportliche Vorführungen des IV./„Deutschland" im Standort Ellwangen.

Motor sport demonstration by IV „Deutschland" in Ellwangen where they were quartered.

Sport und Gesang lieben alle und sie präsentieren sich der Bevölkerung am „Tag der Wehrmacht" (— Tag der offenen Tür —)

Sport and singing are loved by all and they give an exhibition to the public on their open day „The Day of the Wehrmacht"

und die Bevölkerung kam in Massen.

and the public ame in great numbers.

General Dollmann, General-Kdo. Kassel (Heer), besichtigt II./„G".

General Dollmann of the Army (Heer) General Command in Kassel visits II „G".

Ein neues Regiment nach Eingliederung Österreichs — „Der Führer" — (DF) zieht in Wien in die Kaserne Schloß Schönbrunn 1938.

After the incorporation of Austria, a new regiment, „Der Führer" (DF) takes quarters in the Schönbrunn Palace barracks in Vienna 1938.

Fritz von Scholz, SS-Sturmbannführer, Bataillons-Kommandeur im Rgt. „DF" (gefallen).

Fritz von Scholz
Battalion commander in the Regiment „DF" (killed in action).

Regiment „Deutschland" der SS-VT paradiert in Kufstein am 13.3.1938 vor seinem Kommandeur SS-Standartenführer Felix Steiner.

Regiment „Deutschland" of the SS-VT parades in Kufstein on 13.3.1938 before its commander SS Standartenführer Felix Steiner.

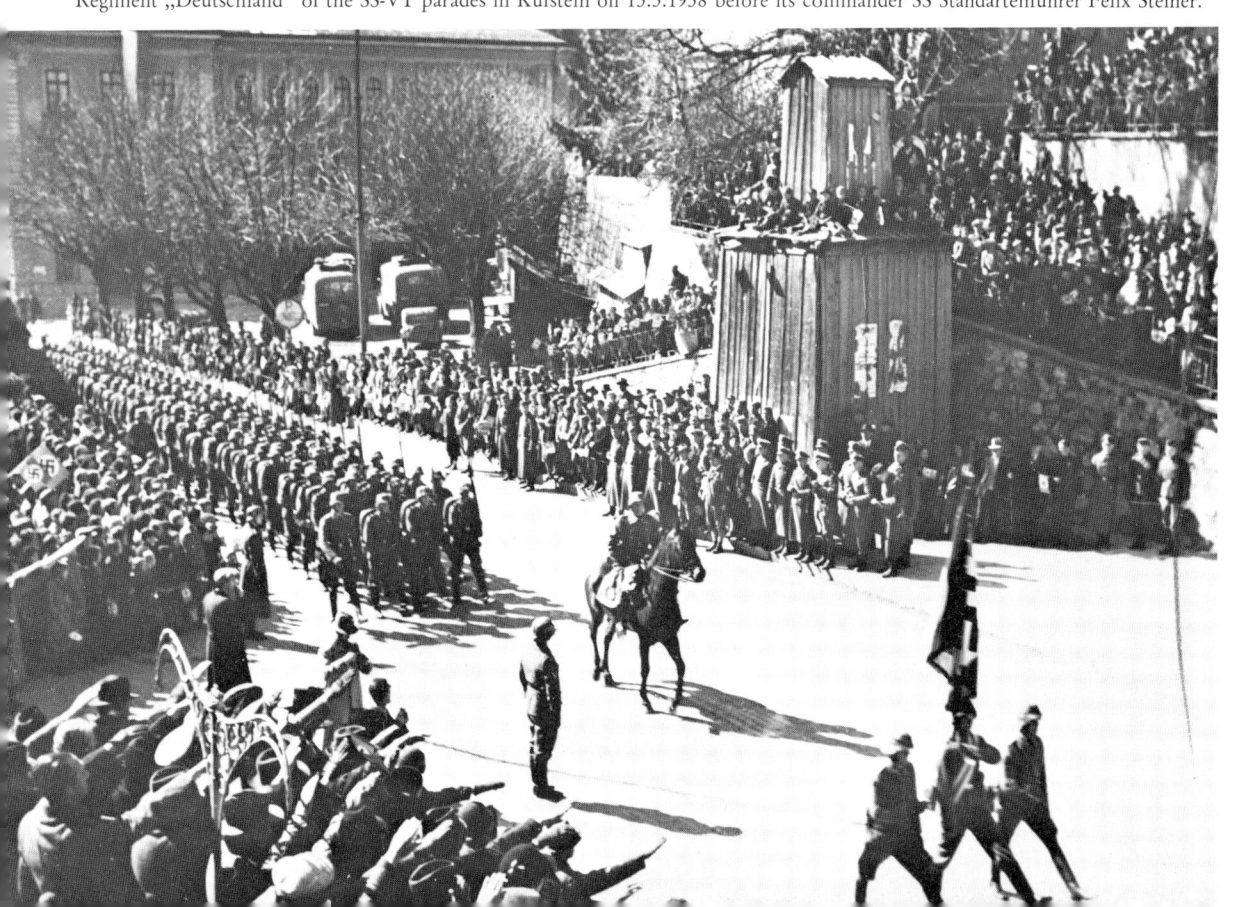

Sudetenland Oktober 1938.

Sudetenland October 1938.

Einmarsch ist befohlen.

They are ordered to march in.

Die Bevölkerung schmückte die Männer vom Bataillon SS-„N" mit Blumen.

The populace adorn the men of Battalion SS-„N" with flowers.

Feldparade 2./SS-„N"
Zugführer SS-Obersturmführer Tychsen (gefallen).

Field parade 2nd SS „N"
Platoon commander SS Obersturmführer Tychsen (killed in action).

Teile des Regimentes „Deutschland" auf dem Hof der Kaserne München.
Damals war das später motorisierte Rgt. noch bespannt und nur teilmotorisiert.

Parts of the Regiment „Deutschland" in the barracks square Munich. The regiment which was later motorized, was at that time still horse drawn and only partly motorized.

III. Bataillon „Germania", vom Manöver zurück, marschiert durch Soltau zum Standort Wolterdingen.

III Battalion „Germania" back from manoeuvres, marches through Soltau to its quarters at Wolterdingen.

Der Große Zapfenstreich.

Military Tattoo („Der Grosse Zapfenstreich").

II./SS-„DF" in Graz 20.4.39 paradiert vor General Dietl vom Heer.

II SS „DF" in Graz 20.4.39, parades before General Dietl of the Army (Heer).

III./„Germania" in neuer Kaserne Radolfzell.

III „Germania" in its new barracks at Radolfzell.

Bataillonsappell des III. Btls. „Germania" in der neuen Kaserne in Radolfzell.

Battalion roll call of the III Battalion „Germania" in the new barracks at Radolfzell.

Reiterfest;
Heer und SS-Verfügungstruppe in der Kaserne SS-„Deutschland" München 1939.

Horse riding festivities;
Army (Heer) and SS Verfügungstruppe in the barracks of SS „Deutschland" Munich 1939.

Am 15.3.39. Besetzung der Tschechoslowakei. Bereitstellung „Germania". Im Schneetreiben marschierten die nun vollmotorisierten Verbände um 6 Uhr über die Grenze und um 9 Uhr war bereits Prag erreicht.

Occupation of Czechoslovakia on 15.3.39. „Germania" assembles in readiness. In driving snow, the units now fully motorized, marched over the frontier at 6 o'clock in the morning and by 9'clock they had already reached Prague.

Generale des Heeres von Blaskowitz und Reinhard schreiten in Iglau am 15.3.39 die Front des Regimentes „Deutschland" ab.

Generals von Blaskowitz and Reinhard of the Army (Heer) pace down the front of the Regiment „Deutschland" in Iglau on 15.3.39.

Alle Einheiten der gesamten SS-Verfügungstruppe waren der Heeresgruppe 4 des Generaloberstens von Blaskowitz unterstellt. In Nürnberg wurde die Waffen-SS allein als verbrecherische Organisation „gebrandmarkt".

All units of the whole Verfügungstruppe were put under the command of Army Group 4 (Heer) under Colonel General von Blaskowitz. In Nürnberg only the Waffen SS were „branded" as a criminal organisation.

Aufstellung des Artillerie-Regimentes der SS-Verfügungstruppe im Sommer 1939. Der erste Kommandeur Oberführer Hansen kam vom Heer (2. von links).

Formation of the Artillery Regiment SS Verfügungstruppe in summer 1939. Oberführer Hansen was the first CO. He was transfered from the Army (2nd left).

Granatwerfertrupp unter Otto Paetsch (gefallen) 15./„Germania".

Trench mortar section under Otto Paetsch (killed in action) 15 „Germania".

SS-Verfügungstruppen bei Absperrungen „gegen" jubelnde Menschenmassen.

SS Verfügungstruppe „restraining" jubilant crowds of people.

Kommandeur Rgt.
„Deutschland",
SS-Standartenführer Steiner,
auf See nach Ostpreußen.

The Commander of the Regiment
„Deutschland", SS-Standartenführer
Steiner, going by sea to East Prussia.

Aufklärungsabteilung lädt am 20.7.1939 in Königsberg
Panzerspähwagen aus

The Reconnaissance Battalion offloads armoured reconnaissance
cars in Königsberg on 20.7.1939

und nimmt an Übungen teil.

and takes part in exercises.

Soldaten des Heeres und der
SS-Verfügungstruppe
lauschen den ernsten Meldungen
vor dem 1.9.39.

Soldiers of the Army (Heer) and the
SS Verfügungstruppe listen to the
grave news reports before 1.9.39.

Abschrift von Abschrift!

Der Oberbefehlshaber des Heeres　　　　　　　　　　　　　　　　　　Berlin, den 20.6.1939
　　2. Abt. (GII A) Gen St d H
　　　　Nr. 1535/39 geh.

Betr.:　Zusammenarbeit des Heeres mit der　　　　　　　　　# Geheim
　　　　　 SS-Verfügungstruppe.

Bezug:　O.K.H. 2. Abt. (III A) Gen St d H
　　　　　 Nr. 919/39 g.Kdos. v. 1.6.39.

An Generalkommando VII. A.K.
　　　　xx.

Der durch den Führererlaß vom 19.5.1939 herbeigeführte Abschluß im Aufbau der **SS-Verfügungstruppe** durch Bildung der SS-Division erfordert in Zukunft eine engere Zusammenarbeit zwischen Heer und SS-Verfügungstruppe als bisher. Auch macht es der vom Führer angeordnete Einsatz der SS-Verfügungstruppe im Rahmen des Feldheeres notwendig, schon im Frieden ein gegenseitiges Verhältnis des Vertrauens und der Kameradschaft zu schaffen, das die Voraussetzung bildet für den gemeinsamen Kampf Schulter an Schulter. Ich ordne daher an, daß durch enge dienstliche und außerdienstliche Verbindung zu den Truppenteilen der SS-Verfügungstruppe die Zusammengehörigkeit zwischen Heer und Verfügungstruppe weitgehendst zu vertiefen ist.

Im Einvernehmen mit dem Reichsführer SS hat sich die Zusammenarbeit auf folgende Gebiete zu erstrecken:

　　Teilnahme der SS-Verfügungstruppe an größeren Truppenübungen, sowie an den
　　Herbstübungen des Heeres im erweiterten Umfang nach Anordnung des O.K.H.
　　Gemeinsame Übungen Heer — SS-Verfügungstruppe auch im kleineren Rahmen
　　(Übungen innerhalb des gemeinsamen Standortes und mit Nachbarstandorten).
　　Teilnahme von Führern der SS-Verfügungstruppe an der Offizierausbildung in den
　　Standorten (z.B. Heranziehung zu Vorträgen, Kriegsspielen, Geländebesprechungen usw.)
　　Gemeinsame sportliche Veranstaltungen (Sportfeste, Offizierschießen).
　　Enge außerdienstliche Verbindung von Offizierkorps und Führerkorps durch Beteiligung
　　an kameradschaftlichen und gesellschaftlichen Veranstaltungen.
　　Betonung der Zusammenarbeit zwischen Heer und SS-Verfügungstruppe durch
　　entsprechende Presseveröffentlichungen (z.B. in den Zeitschriften „Die Wehrmacht" und
　　„Das Schwarze Korps").

Hinsichtlich gegenseitiger Ehrenbezeigungen folgt Befehl. Ich erwarte jedoch, daß schon jetzt das Grußverhältnis entsprechend der Dienststellung der SS-Führer gehandhabt und Anweisung gegeben wird, daß in gemeinsamen Standorten und auf Übungsplätzen oder dort, wo Führer der SS-Verfügungstruppe zu Lehrgängen des Heeres kommandiert sind, diesen dieselben Ehrenbezeigungen erwiesen werden wie Offizieren des Heeres.

Mit der Bildung der SS-Division üben das Besichtigungsrecht über die SS-Verfügungstruppe in meinem Auftrag nur noch die zuständigen Kommandierenden Generale aus. (Nähere Weisung folgt.)

Bei gemeinsamen Übungen steht dem Leitenden des Heeres grundsätzlich auch das Recht zur Kritik und Beurteilung der Truppenteile der SS-Verfügungstruppe zu.

　　　　　　　　　　　　　　　　　　　　　　　　　　　　　gez. v. Brauchitsch.

Generalkommando VII. A.K.　　　　　　　　　　　　　　　　　　　München, den 30.6.1939
(Wehrkreiskommando VII)
　　Az. 34 u. 12 · Ia/Id
　　　　Nr. 6213 geh.

I.　　　　　　　　　　　Verteilt: Kdr. d. Pi. VII
　　　　　　　　　　　　　　　　 pp.

Zusätze des Gen. Kdos.:

II. Die Verfg. Gen. Kdo. VII. A.K. Az. 34 u. 12 Ia/Id Nr. 11 112/38 g. v. 20.12.38, wonach
　　das Besichtigungsrecht der SS-Verfügungstruppe dem Kommandeur der 7. Div. übertragen
　　wurde, wird aufgehoben.
III. Auf enge Zusammenarbeit mit SS-Standarte „Deutschland" wird in erster Linie die 7. Div.
　　angewiesen. Die Div. wird gebeten, alle Übungsvorhaben gem. vorstehender
　　Zusammenstellung rechtzeitig der SS-„D" mitzuteilen wie dies schon bisher geschehen und
　　die SS möglichst zahlreich und häufig zu geeigneten Übungsvorhaben heranzuziehen.
IV. Ich erwarte von allen Angehörigen des Korps, daß der Grußpflicht in straffester Form
　　entsprochen wird.
　　Über Dienstgradabzeichen der SS, sowohl der schwarzen — wie der feldgrauen Uniform,
　　ist die Truppe zu belehren.

　　　　　　　　　　　　　　　　　　　　　　　　　　　　　Der kd. General:
　　　　　　　　　　　　　　　　　　　　　　　　　　　　　　　J.V.
　　　　　　　　　　　　　　　　　　　　　　　　　　　　　gez. Hartemann
　　　　　　　　　　　　　　　　　　　　　　　　　　　　　Generalleutnant.

Copy of a Copy!

The Commander-in-Chief of the Army (Heer)   Berlin, 20.6.1939
   2. Abt. (III A) Gen St d H
     Nr. 1535/39 geh.

Subject: Cooperation between the Army and   **Secret**
the SS-Verfügungstruppe.

Reference: O.K.H. 2. Abt. (III A) Gen St d II
          Nr. 919/39 g.Kdos. v. 1.6.39.

To: Corps Command VII. A.K.

The formation of the SS Division which in accordance with the Führer's Decree of 19.5.1939 concludes the build-up of the SS-Verfügungstruppe, necessitates in the future a closer cooperation than previously between the Army (Heer) and the SS-Verfügungstruppe. Also the Führer's instruction that the SS-Verfügungstruppe is to be operational as part of the Field Army, makes it necessary to foster a relationship of trust and comradeship on both sides in peacetime, which creates the necessary preconditions for their fighting together shoulder to shoulder.

I therefore order that through a close association of the units of the Verfügungstruppe and the Army both on and off duty, there is to be an extensive deepening of collaboration between the Army and the Verfügungstruppe.

With the agreement of the Reichsführer SS, the collaboration is to take place in the following areas:

    Participation by the SS-Verfügungstruppe in the larger military exercises, also in the autumn manoeuvres of the Army to a greater extent as decreed by the Army High Command.

    Joint military exercises of the SS-Verfügungstruppe and the Army on a smaller scale also (exercises in places where they are jointly stationed and with neighbouring garrisons).

    Participation by SS-Verfügungstruppe officers in officer training in the Army garrisons (for example, they should attend lectures, war games, field conferences etc.)

    Joint sporting events (sports meetings, officers' target shooting).

    A close association off duty between both officer corps through participation in events of a comradely and social nature.

    Emphasis on the cooperation between Army and SS-Verfügungstruppe through corresponding press reports (for example, in the newspapers „Die Wehrmacht" and „Das Schwarze Korps").

Orders will follow concerning military salutations. However I expect the relationship between saluting parties to be regulated according to the rank of the SS officers and I expect instructions to be given that in places where there are joint garrisons, on military training grounds or where officers of the SS-Verfügungstruppe are seconded to Army training courses, they are accorded the same salutes as officers of the Army.

With the formation of the SS Division, the right of inspection over the SS-Verfügungstruppe may be exercised on my authority only by the competent Corps Commander. (More detailed instructions follow.)

In joint exercises, the right to make criticism and pass judgement on the units of the SS-Verfügungstruppe rests fundamentally with the Army Command.

                                    signed von Brauchitsch

Corps   Command VII. A.K.   Munich, 30.6.1939
   (Wehrkreiskommando VII)
    Az. 34 u. 12 · Ia/Id
    Nr. 6213 gch.

I.   Distribution: Kdr. d. Pi. VII
                               pp.

Additions by Corps Command:

II. The order, Verfg. Gen. Kdo. VII. A.K. Az. 34 u. 12 Ia/Id nr. 11 112/38 g. of 20.12.38, according to which the right of inspection of the SS Verfügungstruppe was given to the Commander of the 7th Division, is cancelled.

III. The 7th Division in the first instance is required to collaborate closely with the SS Standarte „Deutschland". The Division is requested to inform SS „D" in good time of all exercise plans which are at present drawn up, (which has already happened up to now) and to involve the SS in their plans for suitable military exercises on as many and frequent occasions as possible.

IV. I expect all members of the Corps to perform their duty to salute in the strictest possible manner. The troops are to be given instruction about the SS insignia of rank of both the black and the field-grey uniform.

                                    The Commanding General:
                                               J.V.
                                        signed Hartemann
                                          Lieut. General

Diese gemischte Division setzte sich wie folgt zusammen:
7. Panzerregiment (Heer)
Infanterie-Regiment „Deutschland"
    (SS-Verfügungstruppe)
Artillerie-Regiment
    (SS-Verfügungstruppe)
Nachrichten-Abteilung
    (SS-Verfügungstruppe)
Aufklärungs-Abteilung
    (SS-Verfügungstruppe)
Panzerabwehr-Abteilung 511 (Heer)
Pionier-Bataillon 505 (Heer)
Divisionsnachschubführer
    (SS-Verfügungstruppe)

Im Anschluß an den Polenfeldzug wurde auf dem Truppenübungsplatz Brdy-Wald in der Nähe von Pilsen die Verfügungsdivision aufgestellt.

Lieutenant-Colonel (of the General Staff) von Bernuth
Senior Staff Officer of the Panzer Division Kempf.

This mixed division was composed of the following:
7th Panzer Regiment (Army)
Infantry Regiment „Deutschland"
    (SS Verfügungstruppe)
Artillery Regiment (SS Verfügungstruppe)
Signals Battalion (SS Verfügungstruppe)
Reconnaissance Battalion
    (SS Verfügungstruppe)
Anti-tank Battalion 501 (Army)
Engineers Battalion 505 (Army)
Divisional replacements

Subsequent to the Polish Campaign, the Verfügungs Division was formed at the Brdy Wood military training area near Pilsen.

General Kempf
Kommandeur.

General Kempf
divisional Commander.

Oberstleutnant i.G. von Bernuth
Ia der Panzerdivision Kempf.

Senior Staff Officer

Zwischen Lomza und Bialistock kämpft 10./SS-„Deutschland".
10th/SS „Deutschland" fights between Lomza and Bialistock.

Nördlich von Warschau Rgt. „Deutschland" und Panzerregiment 7 im Angriff.
Regiment „Deutschland" and Panzer Regiment 7 attacking, north of Warsaw.

Kanoniere bringen leichte Feldhaubitze in Stellung.

Gunners emplace a light howitzer.

Übung Regiment "Deutschland".

Training of the Regiment "Deutschland".

Beseitigung einer Baumsperre am 1. Tag bei Peiskretscham durch 1./Pionier-Batl. VT. SS-Obersturmführer Seela.

1 Pioneer Battalion „VT" removing a road block of tree trunks at Peiskretscham on the first day. SS Obersturmführer Seela.

Gefangener polnischer Offizier wird von Aufkl.-Abt. der SS-Verfügungstruppe zum Gefechtsstand gefahren.

Captured Polish officer is driven by he Reconnaissance Battalion of the SS Verfügungstruppe to the command post.

Der erste Gefallene der Pioniere bei Lelow. Bedrückt stehen seine Kameraden am Grab.

At Lelow, the first fatal casualty of the Pioneers. His comrades stand in sadness by his grave.

Zunächst im Fährbetrieb setzt das Pi.Batl. Teile der 4. Infanteriedivision des Heeres über die Weichsel. Dann werden die Fähren eingefahren.

First the Pioneer Battalion transports parts of 4th Infantry Division of the Heer (Army) by ferry over the Weichsel. Then the ferries are docked.

Kriegsbrücke bei Annopol über die Weichsel, erbaut durch Pioniere des Pi.Batl. SS-VT.

Military bridge over the Weichsel at Annopol, built by the engineers of the Pioneer Battalion, SS-VT.

Bau einer Straßenbrücke durch 3. Kp. Pi.Batl. unter SS-Hauptsturmführer Ullrich und SS-Obersturmführer Bunse.

3rd Company Pioneer Battalion under SS Hauptsturmführer Ullrich and SS Obersturmführer Bunse, building a road bridge.

Brücke über die Weichsel bei Annopol, erbaut vom Pionier-Bataillon SS-Verfügungstruppe. Hier setzte die 4. Infanteriedivision des Heeres über.

A bridge over the Weichsel at Annopol, built by the Pioneer Battalion of the SS Verfügungstruppe. The 4th Infantry division of the Army (Heer) crossed here.

Polnische Gefangene gehen über die Weichsel.

Polish prisoners cross the Weichsel.

Bei Zacrozym ergeben sich
polnische Soldaten — die Atmosphäre
ist soldatisch und ohne Haß.

Polish soldiers surrender at Zacrozym —
the atmosphere is as befits soldiers
and there is no hate.

Die 1./Pi.-Batl. tritt aus dem Fort
Mockotowa im infantristischen Einsatz
auf Warschau an (Stoßtrupp).

1 company Pioneer Battalion sets off
from Mockotowa fort in an infantry operation
against Warsaw (assault-detachment).

Alte Wälle des Forts Mockotowa?

The old walls of Mockotowa fort?

Bereitgestellte Panzerspähwagen der SS-Verfügungstruppe.

Armoured scout cars of the SS Verfügungstruppe ready for action.

Modlin kapituliert nach schwerem Kampf —

Modlin surrenders after severe fighting —

freudige Anteilnahme, der Feldzug ist beendet, es geht nach Hause?

general jubilation, the campaign is finished, homeward bound?

Der Westfeldzug der SS-V.-Division.

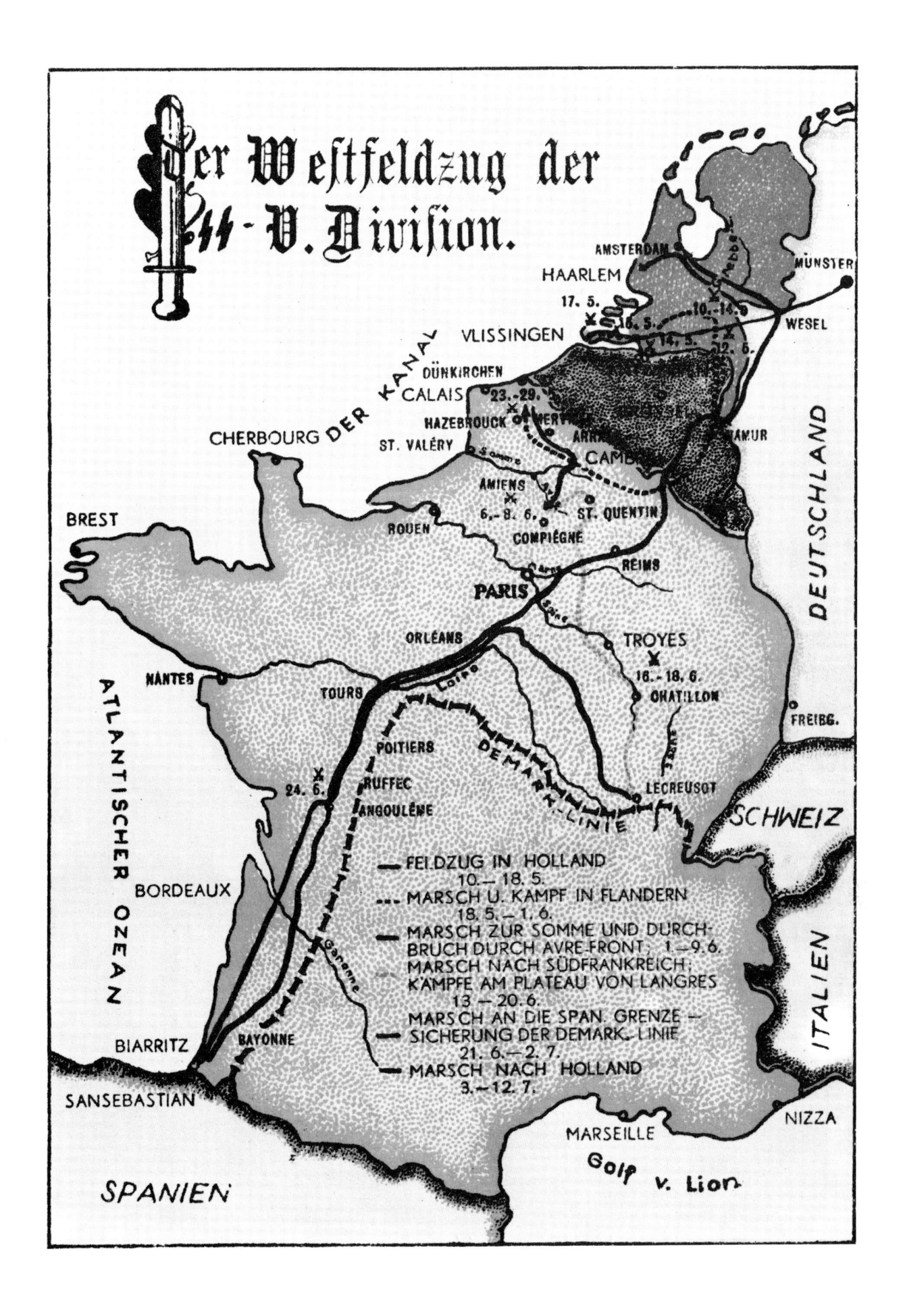

— FELDZUG IN HOLLAND
10.—18. 5.
--- MARSCH U. KAMPF IN FLANDERN
18. 5.—1. 6.
— MARSCH ZUR SOMME UND DURCH-
BRUCH DURCH AVRE-FRONT, 1.—9. 6.
MARSCH NACH SÜDFRANKREICH,
KÄMPFE AM PLATEAU VON LANGRES
13.—20. 6.
MARSCH AN DIE SPAN. GRENZE —
SICHERUNG DER DEMARK. LINIE
21. 6.—2. 7.
— MARSCH NACH HOLLAND
3.—12. 7.

Über die Yssel,
deren Brücken gesprengt sind.

Over the Ijssel, the bridges of which have been blown up.

SS-Verfügungsdivision im Westfeldzug:

SS Verfügungsdivision in the campaign in the West:

Im Vorfeld der Grebbe-Linie in Holland am 12.5.40.

In front of the Grebbe Line in Holland on 12.5.40.

Leichtes Infanteriegeschütz.

A light field gun.

Im Feuer durch Wageningen am 11.5.40 (Yssel).

Under fire through Wageningen on 11.5.40 (Yssel).

Die stark befestigte Grebbe-Linie, die nur unter schweren Verlusten vom Regiment „Der Führer" überwunden werden konnte.

The strongly fortified Grebbe Line which could only be overcome by the Regiment „DF".

Infanteriegeschütze wirken hinter Deckungen.

Infantry guns in operation under cover.

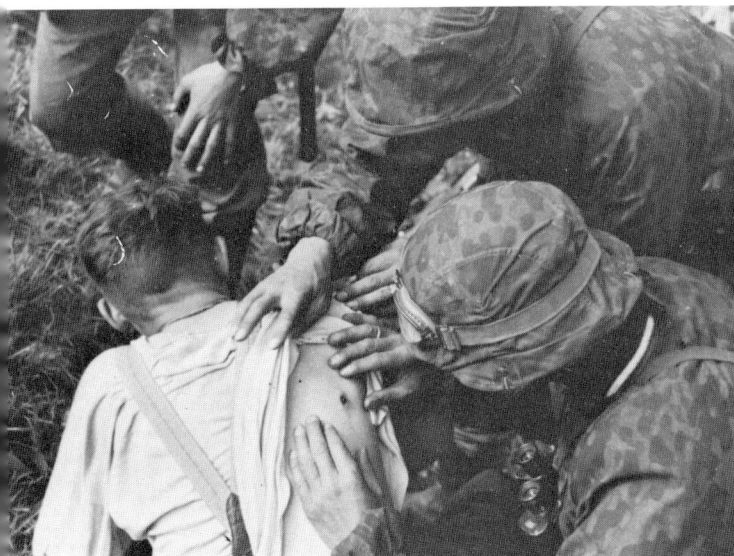

Unsere Sanitäter helfen verwundetem Holländer.

Our medical orderlies help wounded Dutchman.

Nach geglücktem Durchbruch des Regiments „DF".

After a successful break-through by the Regiment „DF".

Divisionskommandeur SS-Gruppenführer und Generalleutnant der Waffen-SS Hausser mit SS-Oberführer Keppler, Kommandeur Regiment „DF".

Divisional CO SS-Gruppenführer and Lieutenant General of the Waffen-SS Paul Hausser with Oberführer Keppler, CO Regiment „DF".

Ihre Gewehre sind in traditioneller Weise deutlich sichtbar in Dreier- oder Vierergruppen ordentlich in einer Position aufgestellt, das ermöglicht ihnen eine rasche Erholung. Die wichtigen Teile der Waffe zeigen nach oben, abgekehrt von Schmutz und Feuchtigkeit.

Their rifles are clearly shown stacked in groups of three or four in the traditional manner that kept them neatly in one position and allowed for their rapid recovery whilst at the same time keeping the important working parts of the weapon off the ground and away from dirt and damp.

Leitfunkstelle in der Gefechtspause.

The main radio post during a break in the fighting.

In Haarlem wird kurze Rast eingelegt

They get in a short rest in Haarlem

dann geht der Marsch rasch weiter.

and then the march rapidly continues.

Panzerspähwagen
unter Untersturmführer Heuer.

Armoured scout car
under Untersturmführer Heuer.

Gefangene Holländer.
Im Vordergrund rechts
Obersturmbannführer Wäckerle
(gefallen).

Dutch prisoners.
In the foreground on the right
Obersturmbannführer Wäckerle
(killed in action).

Minenräumen durch Pioniere.

Pioneers clear mines.

Neue Befehle erwartend in der Deckung —

Waiting under cover for new orders —

und es geht stetig vorwärts.

and all the time on the advance.

Eine außerordentliche Zahl der verschiedensten Beutewaffen, oft unzerstört, fielen in die Hände der Männer der V-Division.

An extraordinary number of captured weapons of all kinds, often undamaged, fell into the hands of the men of the V-Division.

Erste Auszeichnungen.

First decorations.

Das Eiserne Kreuz.

The Iron Cross.

54

SS-Hauptsturmführer Elmenreich am La Basseé-Kanal fiedelt aus Freude über den Erfolg.

SS Hauptsturmführer Elmenreich rejoices over their success by playing his fiddle at La Bassée Canal.

SS-Obersturmführer Fritz Vogt erhält das Ritterkreuz für seine Taten und die der Aufklärungs-Abteilung.

SS-Obersturmführer Fritz Vogt receives the Knight's Cross for his actions and those of the Reconnaissance Battalion.

Sie hält still und alle lachen —
aber melken muß man können.

She kept still and everyone laughed —
but you have to know to milk.

→

Nächste Seite
Panzerjäger

Next page
Anti-tank gunners

Flüchtlinge.

Refugees.

Der distinguierte Kradmelder Hirsch hat
den Stahlhelm eingetauscht.

The distinguished despatch rider Hirsch has
exchanged his steel helmet.

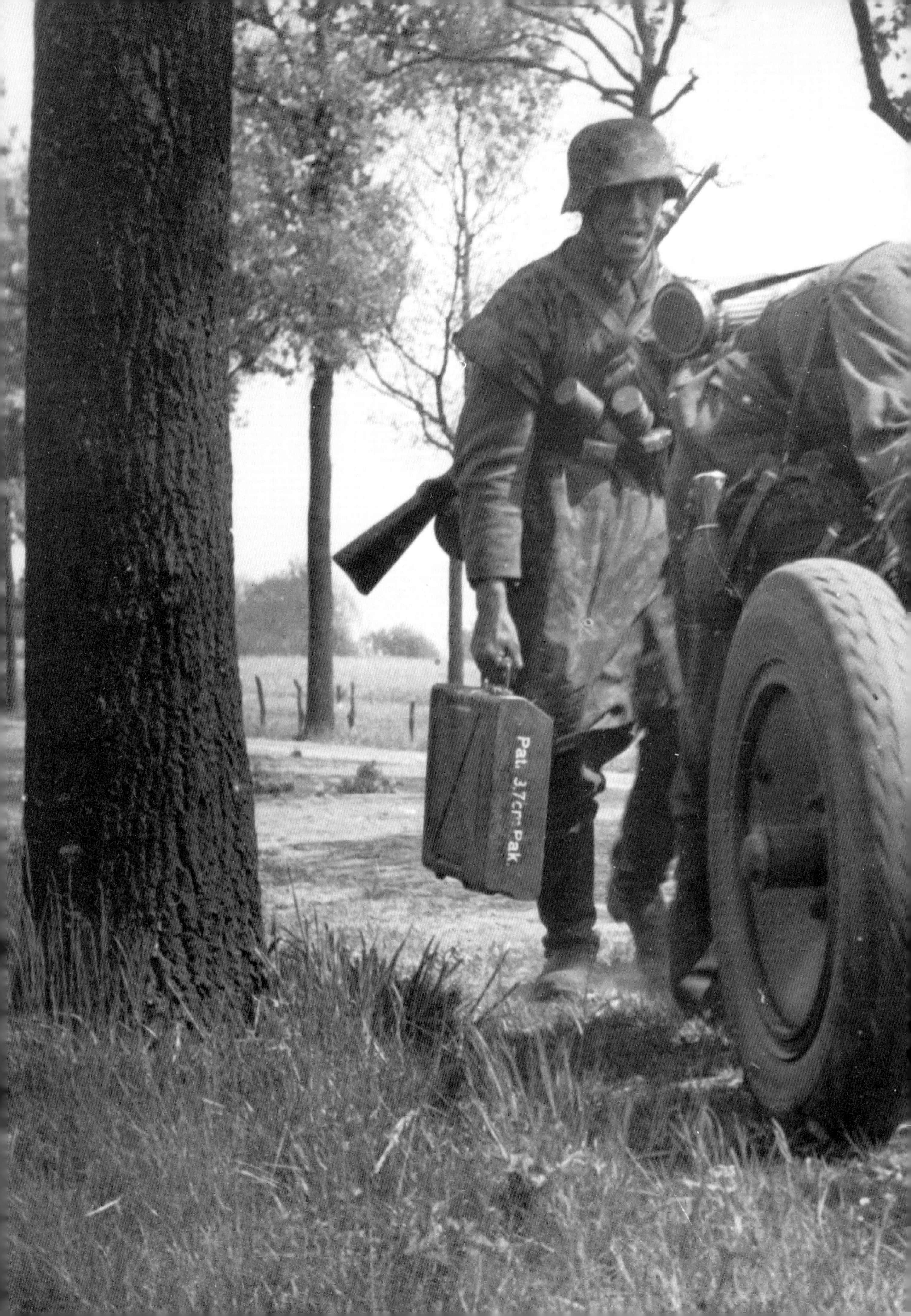
Pat. 3,7cm Pak.

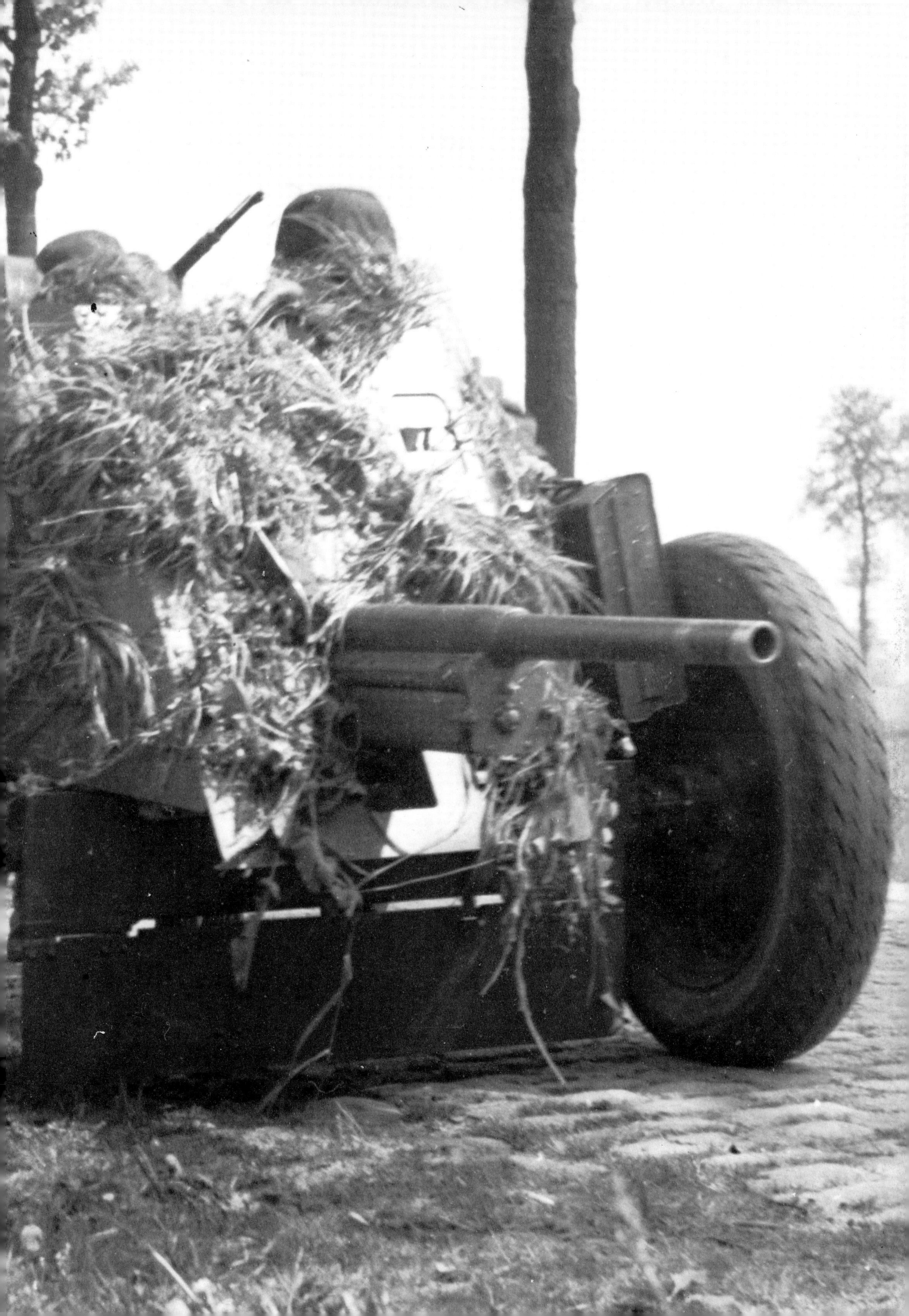

Auch tapfere Soldaten kennen die Angst.

Brave soldiers know fear too.

Rasch in Stellung!

Quickly in position!

Sofort im Feuerkampf!

Firing instantaneously!

Bei Bailleul und Aire wurden mehr als 100 französische Panzer von den Soldaten der SS-Verfügungstruppe vernichtet und erbeutet.
Near Bailleul and Aire more than 100 French tanks were destroyed by soldiers of the SS Verfügungstruppe and captured.

Im Ortsgefecht.

House to house fighting.

SS-Untersturmführer Professor Petersen als Kriegsberichter.

SS Untersturmführer Professor Petersen as a war correspondent.

Gefangene Engländer.

English prisoners.

Englischer Panzerspähwagen
außer Gefecht.

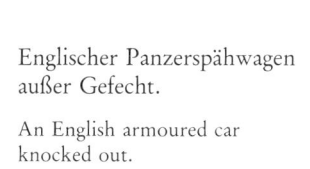

An English armoured car
knocked out.

Franzosen ergeben sich
auf der Insel Zeeland.

Frenchmen surrender
on the island of Zeeland.

Viele fliehen
in Zivil.

Many flee
in civilian clothes.

50 französische Panzer brechen beim II. Batl. DF in
Aire durch, umfassen 2 Kompanien,
dann setzt der Gegenstoß ein

50 French tanks break through near II Battalion „DF" in
Aire and encircle 2 companies.
Then the counter attack starts

und das I. Bataillon vernichtet
die feindl. Panzer.

I Battalion which destroyed the enemy tanks.

Unsere Artillerie hilft.

Our artillery helps.

Feuer!
Fire!

Gefechtspause.
Break in the fighting.

Feindpanzer
aus der Nähe gesehen . . .

Enemy tanks
seen at close quarters . . .

La Basseé-Kanal —
jenseits der Feind.

La Bassée Canal —
on the other side is the enemy.

I./SS „D" im Angriff
über den Kanal.

I SS „D" attacking across the canal.

Gefangene Engländer
bei Merville.

English prisoners
near Merville.

Ein verwundeter Kamerad.

A wounded comrade.

Marschhalt —
übermüdete Kradmelder
nutzen jeden Halt
zum Schlaf.

A halt during the march —
exhausted despatch riders
utilize every halt
for sleeping.

Beute-Munition am Wege.

Captured ammunition by the road.

Kradschützen der Aufklärungs-
Abteilung auf dem Vormarsch neben
Gefangenenkolonnen.

Motorcycle infantry of the Reconnaissance
Battalion advancing next to columns
of prisoners.

Am Meer —
Bergung einer Seemine.

By the sea —
Salvaging a mine.

An der französisch-spanischen Grenze.
On the French-Spanish frontier.

Flüchtlingen wird mit Benzin die Heimkehr ermöglicht.

Refugees get petrol enabling them to return home.

Nach all der Anstrengung — baden im Atlantik.

After all the exertion — a bathe in the Atlantic.

Unser Hauptmann auf 'ner Kuh —
alles lacht vergnügt dazu.
Der Krieg ist aus?

Our captain's sitting on a cow —
Everybody's laughing now.
Is the war over?

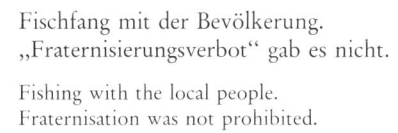

Fischfang mit der Bevölkerung.
„Fraternisierungsverbot" gab es nicht.

Fishing with the local people.
Fraternisation was not prohibited.

Rasur im Rückspiegel.
SS-Hauptsturmführer Milius.

Shaving in the driving mirror.
SS Hauptsturmführer Milius.

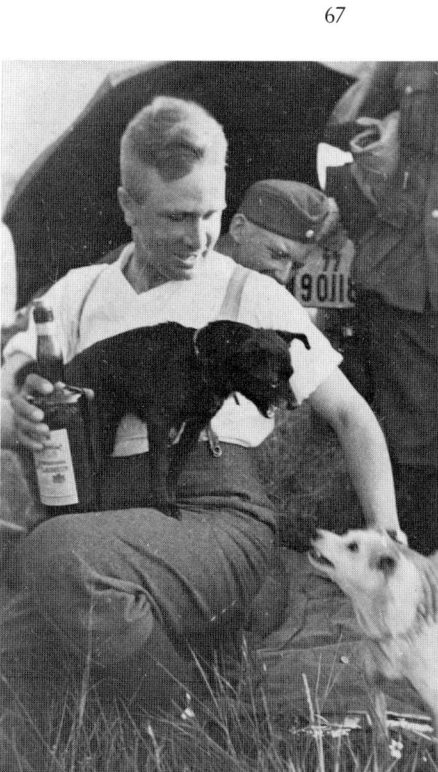

Eifersüchtig verteidigt Fifi
den Platz.
Die Tierliebe war beim
Landser allgemein.

Fifi defends the place jealously.
Love of animals was general
among the soldiers.

Auch Ovambo kam nochmal davon.

Ovambo came through once again too.

Parade vor dem Kommandeur der Division —
Die Ehrenkompanie rückt an.

A parade in front of the commander of the division —
The guard of honour approaches.

SS-Gruppenführer und Generalleutnant
der Waffen-SS Paul Hausser
mit 1. Generalstabsoffizier Ostendorff,
Adjutant Mühlenkamp
und 1. Ordonnanzoffizier Mäcker.

SS Gruppenführer und Lieutenant General
of the Waffen SS Paul Hausser
with the senior staff officer Ostendorff,
Adjutant Mühlenkamp
and the senior orderly officer Mäcker.

Spanische Offiziere
mit dem Kommandeur
des SS-Regiments „Deutschland",
Felix Steiner.

Spanish officers
with the commander of the
SS Regiment „Deutschland",
Felix Steiner.

Sie und viele andere
mußten ihr Leben lassen —

They and many others
had to relinquish their lives —

Ehrenkompanie unter SS-Hauptsturmführer Harzer in Braunschweig zum Volkstrauertag 1940. Diese Kompanie wurde von Standartenjunkern des Führerlehrganges Braunschweig 40/41 gebildet.

Guard of honour under SS Hauptsturmführer Harzer in Brunswick on the National Day of Mourning 1940. This company was established by officer cadets of the course of instruction at Brunswick 40/41.

Bilder der Kriegsberichter in der Heimat

Photographs taken by war — correspondents are shown at home

und im Frontkino.

and in military cinemas.

Kampf um eine Ortschaft. Kriegsnahe Übung. Regiment „DF" 1940.

The battle for a village. Realistic combat exercises. Regiment „DF" early 1940.

Der Südostfeldzug

The campaign in south-east Europe

Der Feldzug gegen Jugoslawien dauerte nur 7 Tage für die Division „Das Reich". Regiment „Deutschland" stößt auf Alibunar.

The campaign against Yugoslavia lasted only 7 days for the Division „Das Reich". Regiment „Deutschland" pushes towards Alibunar.

Die Straßensperre ist kein ernsthaftes Hindernis.

The road block is not a serious obstruction.

Gefangener jugoslawischer Offizier

A captured Yugoslavian officer

und seine Soldaten.

and his soldiers.

Behelfsbrücke neben der gesprengten Donaubrücke bei Belgrad.

A temporary bridge next to the blown-up Danube bridge at Belgrade.

Der Divisionskommandeur Hausser mit Adjutant SS-Hauptsturmführer Weidinger und SS-Untersturmführer Hinze, Chef 4. Kompanie, Kradschützenbataillon, setzen über die Donau.

The divisional commander Hausser with adjutant SS Hauptsturmführer Weidinger und SS Untersturmführer Hinze, commander of 4th Company, Motorcycle Battalion, cross the Danube.

Am 14.4.41 um 18.45 Uhr fällt Belgrad im Handstreich — durch SS-Hauptsturmführer Klingenberg (gefallen 1945). Er ist nur mit einem Stoßtrupp in der Stadt, doch sie wird übergeben.

On 14.4.41 at 18.45 Belgrade fell to a surprise attack — SS Hauptsturmführer Klingenberg (killed in action 1945). He was only in the town with a small assault detachment but it still surrendered.

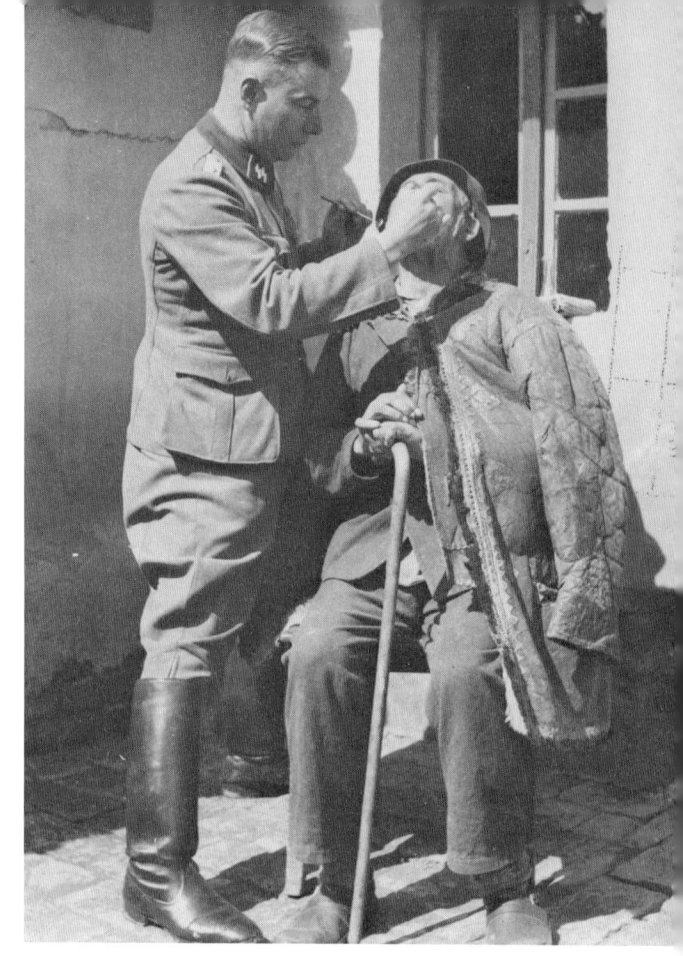

Truppenzahnarzt und serbischer Schäfer.

The troops' dentist and a Serbian shepherd.

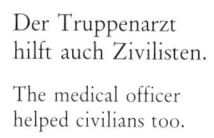

Ein Bauer aus dem Banat.

A farmer from the Banat.

Der Truppenarzt hilft auch Zivilisten.

The medical officer helped civilians too.

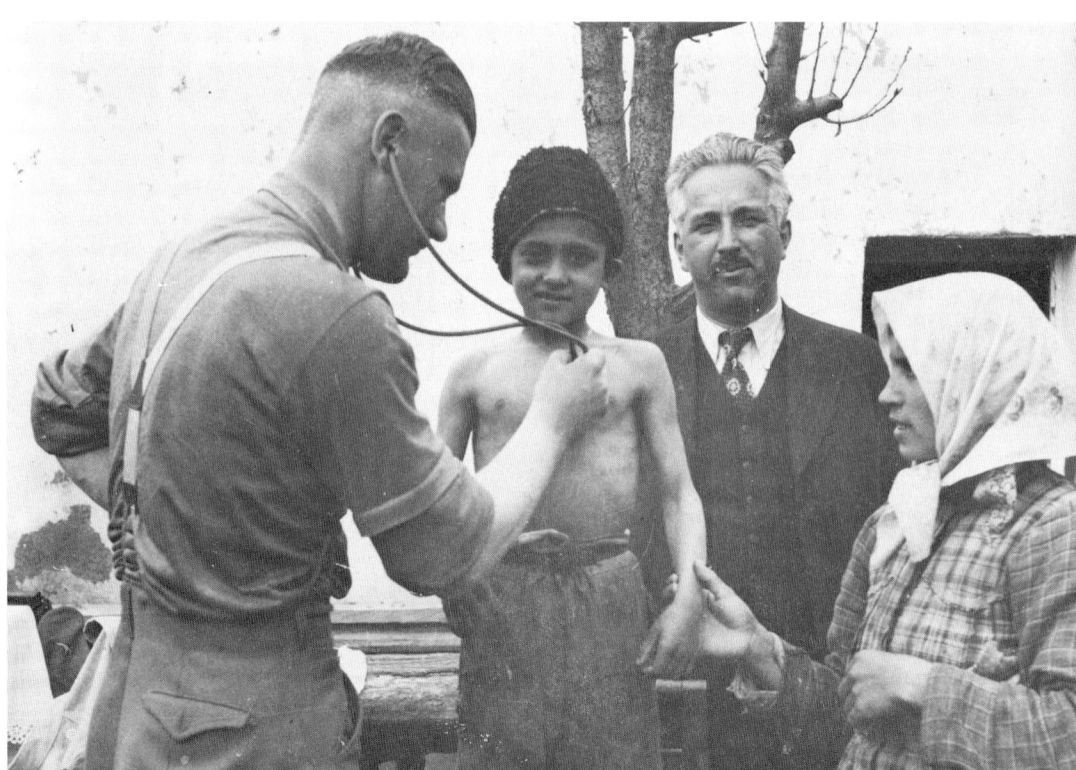

Der 1. Ostertag 1941
wird überall
mit der Bevölkerung gefeiert.

Everywhere the first day of Easter 1941
was celebrated with the local population.

Die Truppe feiert „Führergeburtstag".

The troops celebrate the Führer's birthday.

Ostertanz in Alibunar.

An Easter dance in Alibunar.

Die Bevölkerung
bringt Blumen.

The people bring flowers.

Zerstörte Hängebrücke
bei Belgrad 14.4.41.

A destroyed suspension bridge
at Belgrade 14.4.41.

75

Ruhetage.

A break for some days.

Der Führer und Oberste Befehlshaber F.H.Qu., den 18.12.40
der Wehrmacht
OKW/WFSt/Abt. L (I) Nr. 33 408/40 g.K. Chefs.

Weisung Nr. 21
Fall Barbarossa

Die deutsche Wehrmacht muß darauf vorbereitet sein, auch vor Beendigung des Krieges gegen England, **Sowjetrußland in einem schnellen Feldzug niederzuwerfen** (Fall Barbarossa). Die Vorbereitungen der Oberkommandos sind auf folgender Grundlage zu treffen:

I.) **Allgemeine Absicht:**

Die im westlichen Rußland stehende Masse des russischen **Heeres** soll in kühnen Operationen unter weitem Vortreiben von Panzerkeilen vernichtet, der Abzug kampfkräftiger Teile in die Weite des russischen Raumes verhindert werden. In rascher Verfolgung ist dann eine Linie zu erreichen, aus der die russische Luftwaffe reichsdeutsches Gebiet nicht mehr angreifen kann. Das Endziel der Operation ist die Abschirmung gegen das asiatische Rußland aus der allgemeinen Linie Wolga — Archangelsk. So kann erforderlichenfalls das letzte Rußland verbleibende Industriegebiet am Ural durch die Luftwaffe ausgeschaltet werden.

II.) **Voraussichtliche Verbündete und deren Aufgaben:**

....

III.) **Die Führung der Operationen:**

A.) Heer (in Genehmigung der mir vorgetragenen Absichten):

In dem durch die Pripjetsümpfe in eine südliche und eine nördliche Hälfte getrennten Operationsraum ist der Schwerpunkt **nördlich** dieses Gebietes zu bilden. Hier sind 2 Heeresgruppen vorzusehen.

Der südlichen dieser beiden Heeresgruppen — Mitte der Gesamtfront — fällt die Aufgabe zu, mit besonders starken Panzer- und mot. Verbänden aus dem Raum um und nördlich Warschau vorbrechend die feindlichen Kräfte in Weißrußland zu zersprengen. Dadurch muß die Voraussetzung geschaffen werden für das Eindrehen von starken Teilen der schnellen Truppen nach Norden, um im Zusammenwirken mit der aus Ostpreußen in allgemeiner Richtung Leningrad operierenden nördlichen Heeresgruppe die im Baltikum kämpfenden feindlichen Kräfte zu vernichten. Erst nach Sicherstellung dieser vordringlichen Aufgabe, welcher die Besetzung von Leningrad und Kronstadt folgen muß, sind die Angriffsoperationen zur Besitznahme des wichtigen Verkehrs- und Rüstungszentrums Moskau fortzuführen.

Nur ein überraschend schnell eintretender Zusammenbruch der russischen Widerstandskraft könnte es rechtfertigen, beide Ziele gleichzeitig anzustreben.

Bei der südlich der Pripjet-Sümpfe angesetzten Heeresgruppe ist der Schwerpunkt im Raum von Lublin in allgemeiner Richtung Kiew zu bilden, um mit starken Pz.-Kräften schnell in die tiefe Flanke und den Rücken der russischen Kräfte vorzugehen und diese dann im Zuge des Dnjepr aufzurollen.

Sind die Schlachten südlich bzw. nördlich der Pripjet-Sümpfe geschlagen, ist im Rahmen der Verfolgung anzustreben:

im Süden die frühzeitige Besitznahme des wehrwirtschaftlich wichtigen Donez-Beckens,

im Norden das schnelle Erreichen von Moskau.

Die Einnahme dieser Stadt bedeutet politisch und wirtschaftlich einen entscheidenden Erfolg, darüber hinaus den Ausfall des wichtigen Eisenbahnknotenpunktes.

gez. Adolf Hitler.

Das Schicksal nahm seinen Lauf.

The Führer and Supreme Head Führer H.Q., 18.12.40
of the Armed Forces
OKW/WFSt/Abt. L (1) Nr. 33 408/40 g.k. Chefs.

Directive No. 21
Operation Barbarossa

The German Wehrmacht must be prepared, even before the ending of the war with England, **to overthrow Soviet Russia in a swift campaign** (Operation Barbarossa).
The preparations of the High Commands are to be effected on the following basis:

I.) **General Plan:**

The mass of the Russian **Army** positioned in Western Russia is to be destroyed in bold operations involving deep penetration by panzer spearheads, and the withdrawal of effective fighting forces to the open spaces of the Russian regions is to be prevented.

In swift pursuit, a line is then to be reached from which the Russian Air Force can no longer attack the German Reich area. The final objective of the operation is to shield against Asiatic Russia from the general line Volga-Archangelsk. Then if required, the last industrial area remaining to the Russians in the Urals can be put out of action by the Luftwaffe.

II.) **Prospective allies and their tasks:**

....

III.) **Command of the operations:**

A.) H e e r (Army) (in approval of plans submitted to me):

The area of operations is divided into northern and southern halves by the Pripet marshes and the main point of attack is to be **to the north** of this area. Two Army Groups are to be assigned here. Of these two Army Groups, the one to the south — the centre of the whole front — breaking out of the area around and to the north of Warsaw with specially strong panzer and motorized forces, has the task of routing the enemy forces in White Russia. It is essential that the conditions are thereby created for strong detachments of the fast moving troops to turn northwards in order to destroy the enemy forces fighting in the Baltic area, in cooperation with the northern Army Group operating out of East Russia in the general direction of Leningrad. Only after the accomplishment of this priority task, which must be followed by the occupation of Leningrad and Kronstadt, are offensive operations for securing the important communications and armaments centre of Moscow, to be continued.

Only if Russian resistance started to collapse with unexpected speed, could there be justification for attempting both objectives at the same time.

The Army Group operating south of the Pripet marshes is to make the main point of its thrust in the Lublin area in the direction of Kiev in order to advance rapidly with strong armoured forces deep into the flank and rear of the Russian forces and then to roll them up along the course of the Dnieper.

If the battles are successful, north or south of the Pripet marshes, they should be followed up by:

in the south, the early occupation of the important armaments manufacturing Donez basin,

in the north, the rapid attainment of Moscow.

The capture of this town would mean politically and economically a decisive success and moreover the loss of an important railway junction.

signed Adolf Hitler.

The fate takes its course.

Noch ist in der Bereitstellung
nichts von Krieg zu spüren.

There is still no hint of war in the assembly area.

Alle hören am 21.6.41 die Kriegsfanfare.
Hauptsturmführer Wisliceny mit seiner 8. Kompanie/IR 11.

Everyone listens to the military fanfare.
Hauptsturmführer Wisliceny with his 8th Company/IR 11.

Kompanie-Funktrupp.
Radio squad of the company.

Infantrie geht
in Bereitstellung.

Infantry moring
in readiness.

Fahrzeuge des Divisionsstabes getarnt.

Divisional staff vehicles camouflaged.

Männer der Fernsprechkompanie beim Bau der Leitungen.

Men of the Telephone Company laying the cables.

Kommandeur der Aufklärungs-Abteilung der Division „Das Reich",
SS-Hauptsturmführer Hannes Mühlenkamp bei der Besichtigung.

Commander of the Reconnaissance Battalion of the Division „Das Reich",
SS Hauptsturmführer Mühlenkamp making an inspection.

Der Kommandeur
des Artillerie-Regiments
der Division „Das Reich"
SS-Oberführer Hansen.

Commander of the
Artillery Regiment of the
Division „Das Reich"
SS Oberführer Hansen.

Panzerspähzug stößt über die Brücke von Buchowice über den Bug — an der Spitze ein 8-Rad-Spähpanzer.

An armoured reconnaissance group presses on across the bridge at Buchowice over the Bug —
headed by a heavy armoured ‚eight wheeler'.

Motorisierter Spähtrupp

Motorized reconnaissance detachment

Kradschützen pflegen
während Marschpausen zu ruhen.
Kleine Unbequemlichkeiten
werden in Kauf genommen.

Motorcycle infantry make a habit
of resting during breaks in the march.
They put up with small discomforts.

An der Beresina am 29.6.41 —
15. Kompanie „DF" und Aufklärungs-Kompanie

On the Beresina on 29.6.41 —
15th Company „DF" and the Reconnaissance Company

— wenig später erhält die Spitze Feuer.
— a little later the spearhead draws fire.

Der Kommandeur der
Aufklärungsabteilung
auf dem Divisions-
Gefechtsstand.

The commander of the
Reconnaissance Battalion
at the divisional
command post.

Abgeschossener 8-Rad-Panzerspähwagen
der Aufklärungs-Abteilung
vor der Brücke von Buchowicze.

A knocked-out eight-wheeled armoured car
of the Reconnaissance Battalion
before the bridge of Buchowicze.

Vormarsch Juni 1941
auf allen Wegen.

Advance on all routes,
June 1941.

Am 4.7.41
geht es über eine Behelfsbrücke,
die über die Beresina führt.

On 4.7.41, a temporary bridge is used,
which crossed the Beresina.

Diese Brücke über die Beresina
bei Jaknitze wurde mit 300 Russen
und einem SS-Sturmgeschütz gesprengt.
Der Geschützführer Telkamp
und seine Besatzung überlebten.

This bridge over the Beresina at Jacknitze
was blown up with 300 Russians
and an SS SP assault gun.
The gun commander Telkamp
and his crew survived.

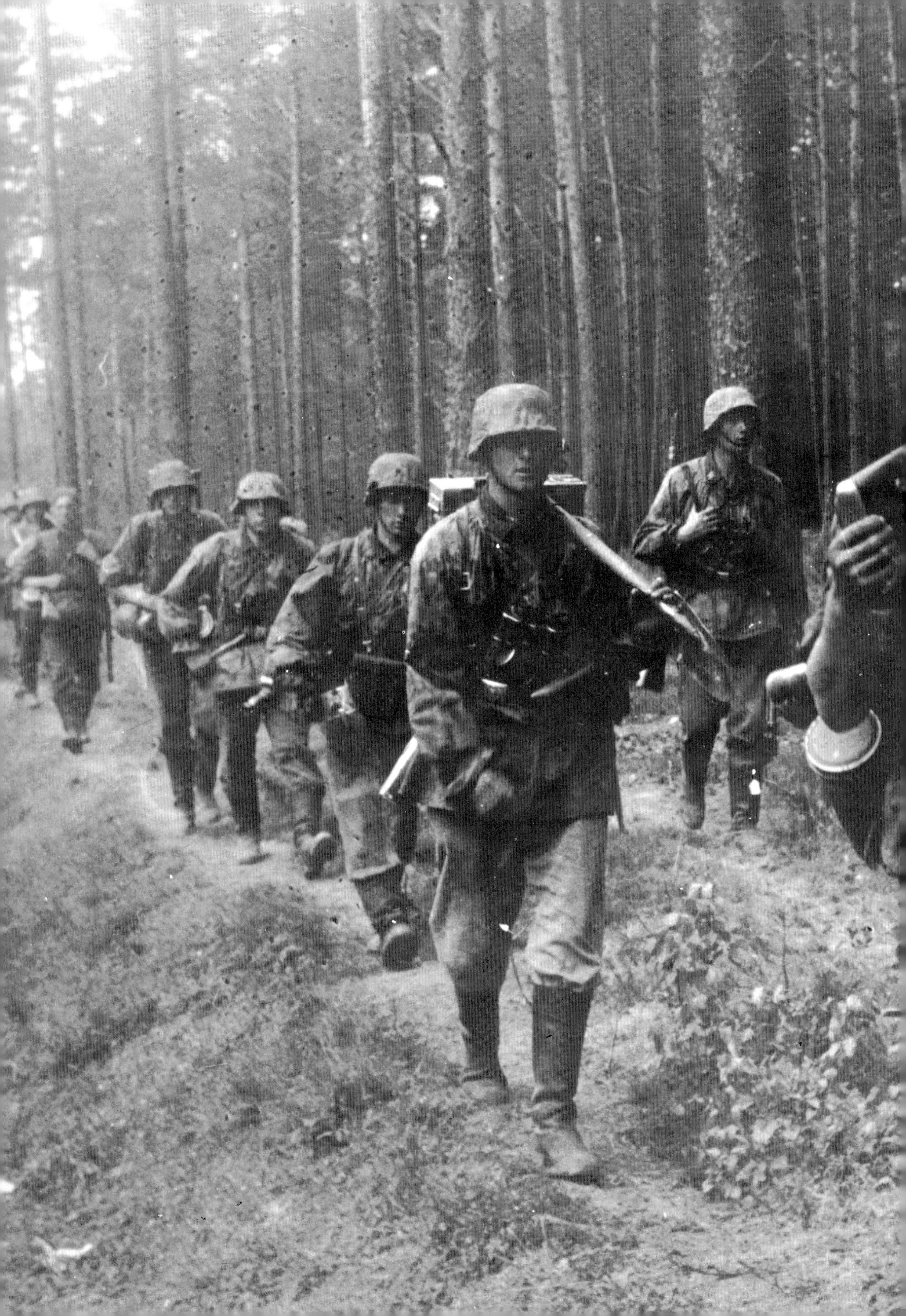

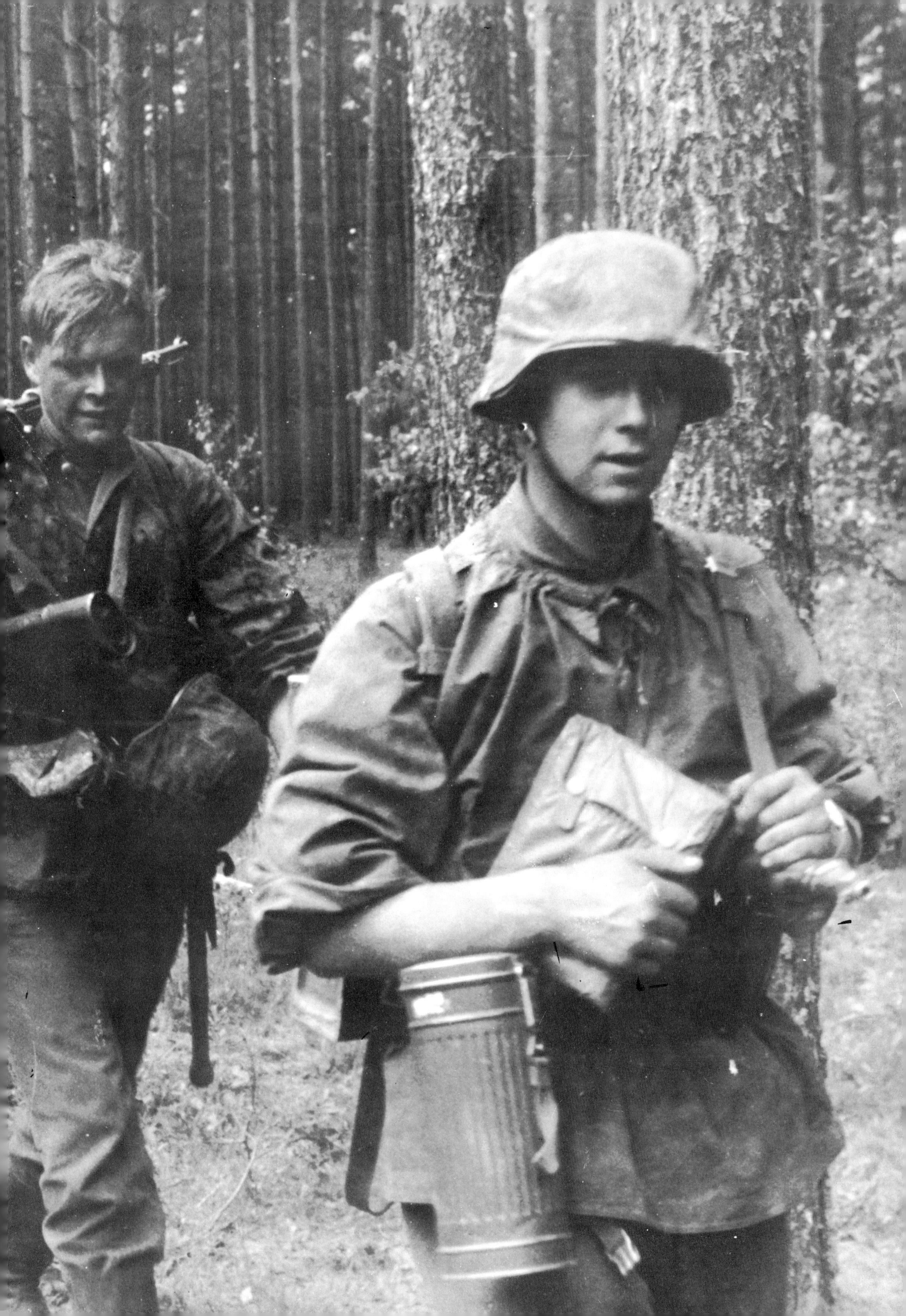

5. (schw.) Kradschützen-Batl. „Das Reich".
Kp. Truppführer Weiß neben dem Fahrer.
„G" = Gruppe Guderian.

5th (heavy) Motorcycle Battalion „Das Reich".
Company commander Weiss next to the driver.
„G" = Army Group Guderian.

Erbeutete
russische Feldküche.

A captured
Russian field kitchen.

Behelfsstege
über zerstörte Brücke.

Emergency bridge
at the destroyed bridge.

Es ging flott voran,
und die Bewohner
waren nicht feindlich.

The advance was brisk and the local
inhabitants were not unfriendly.

Führer des Divisionsstabes mit dem
Ia SS-Obersturmbannführer Ostendorff.

Commander of the divisional staff
with the senior staff officer SS Obersturmbannführer Ostendorff.

Funkstelle der Division ist tätig.

The divisional radio post in operation.

Hier arbeitet die Führungsstaffel

This is where the command staff works

und die „Schreibstube" der Division.

and the „office" of the division.

Durch die Furt — Russen müssen helfen.   Through the ford — the Russians have to help.

Infanterie-Pioniere setzen im Morgengrauen über den Strom.

Pioneer infantry cross the river at dawn.

Beutewaffen
aller Arten.

Captured weapons of all kinds.

Befehlsausgabe am Gefechtsstand II./A.R. „Das Reich". SS-Sturmbannführer Jochen Ruhmor — Kdr. II. A.R. 2 — (gefallen 1945).

Issuing of orders at the command post of II Art. Reg. „Das Reich".
SS Sturmbannführer Jochen Ruhmor — commander of II A.R. 2 — (killed in action 1945).

Russische Gefangene —
sie kümmern sich um einen Jungen.

Russian prisoners — looking after a young boy.

Reste eines „Martin"-Bombers der Roten Luftmacht.

The remains of a „Martin" bomber of the red airforce.

Am Pruth und in der Nähe der Brücke fiel fast die gesamte 2. Pionierkompanie mit Hauptsturmführer Walter Maasch.

Almost the whole 2. pioneer company with Hauptsturmführer Walter Maasch fell at Pruth and in the area around the bridge.

72 tote Pioniere.

Im Hinterhalt grausam bis auf den letzten Mann von den Sowjets niedergemacht.

72 dead pioneers.

Cruelly slayed by the Soviets lying in ambush.

MG in Stellung.   An MG in position.

Infanterie in Bereitstellung.   Infantry in readiness.

Das Ziel ist erreicht.   The objective ist reached.

Diese haben uns die Flieger „abgenommen".

96   These ones have been „taken from us" from the air.

Zerstörte russische Panzer säumen die Vormarschwege.   Destroyed Russian tanks line the routes of the advance.

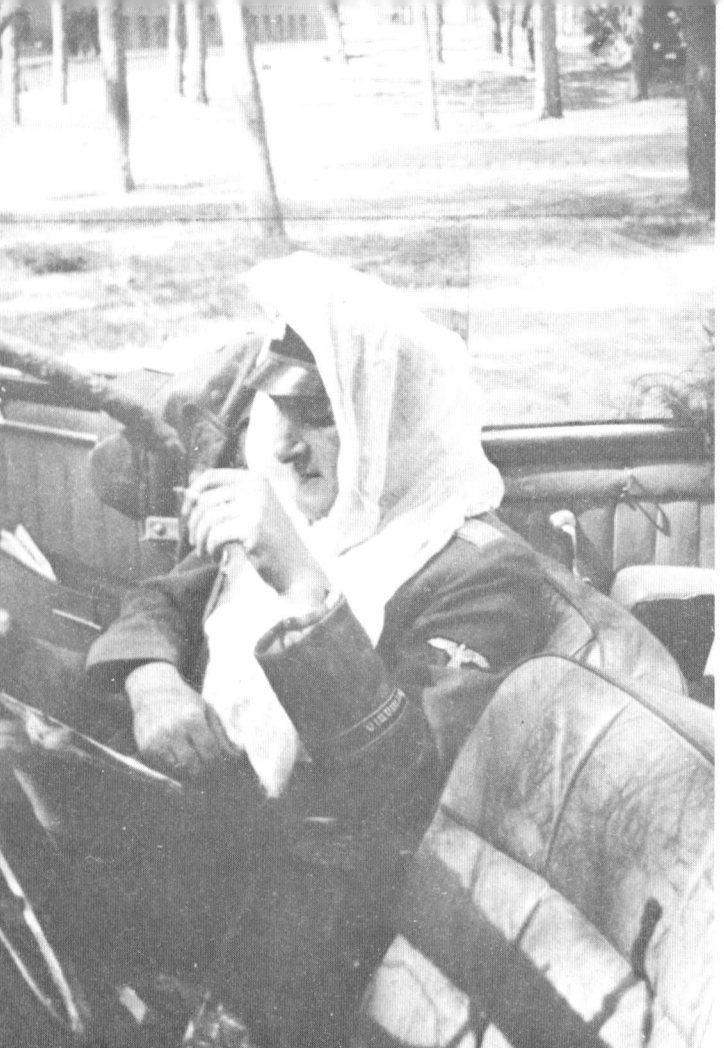

SS-Sturmbannführer Kunstmann
2. Generalstabsoffizier mit Mückenschleier (gefallen 1943).

SS-Sturmbannführer Kunstmann
second staff officer with mosquito-net (killed in action 1943).

Wasser! — Die Männer waren in Staub eingehüllt.

Water! — The men were caked with dust.

Hier sind wir! (Fliegertücher)   We are here! (An aerial recognition panel).

Der Kommandeur
der Kradschützen,
SS-Hauptsturmführer
Klingenberg, heftet einem
tapferen Soldaten
das Eiserne Kreuz
1. Klasse an.

Commander of the
motorcycle infantry,
SS Hauptsturmführer
Klingenberg pins the Iron Cross
1st Class on a courageous soldier.

Im Fährbetrieb werden von den Pionieren mit großen an Sturmbooten gekoppelten Floßsäcken die Männer der Division übergesetzt.

The pioneers ferried the men of the division across, in huge rubber dinghies attached to assault crafts.

Übersetzverkehr mit Floßsack-Einfachfähre.

Rubber dinghy ferry traffic.

Kanoniere in einer Feuerpause.

Gunners during a break in the firing.

Schweres Infanteriegeschütz im Feuerkampf.   Heavy field gun firing in battle.

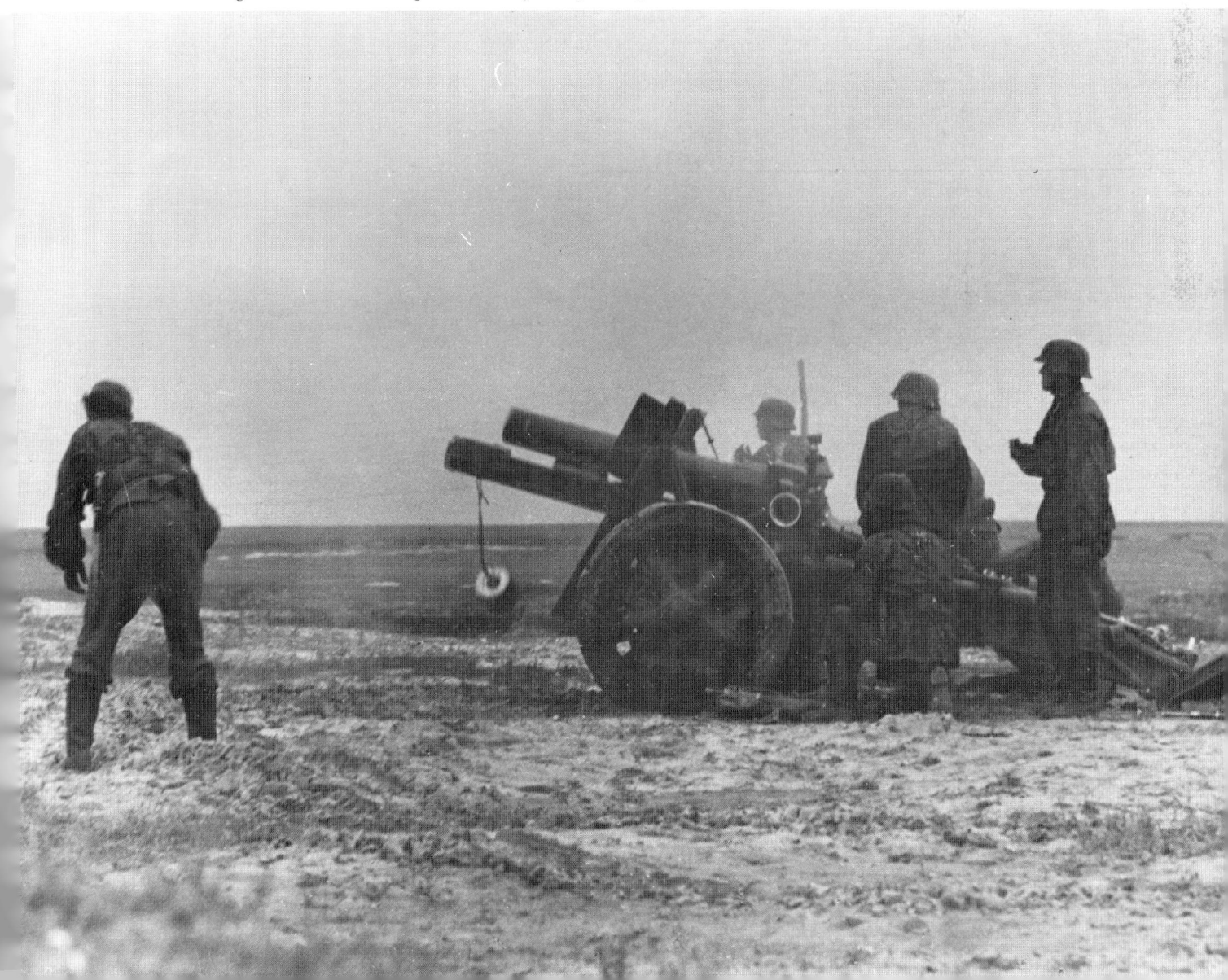

Panzer gemeldet —
Pak schnell nach vorn.
Die 3,7 cm war das
„Heeresanklopfgerät".

A panzer is reported — the anti-tank gun is brought quickly forward. The 3,7 cm Pak was The Army's „door knocker" (translator's note: because it was not powerful enough to penetrate the tank armour).

Munition war noch genug

There was still enough ammunition

Festgefahren im Sand.

They got bogged down in sand.

Eingebrachter Gefangener wartet auf Verhör, die Männer bleiben kampfbereit.

A prisoner is brought in and waits to be interrogated, the men remain in an state of combat readiness.

nächste Seite:
und die 2 cm Flak nahm die gegnerische Infanterie an.

next page:
and the 2 cm Flak took on the enemy infantry.

Kurze Rast einer Kradschützen-Kompanie.

A short rest for the motorcycle company.

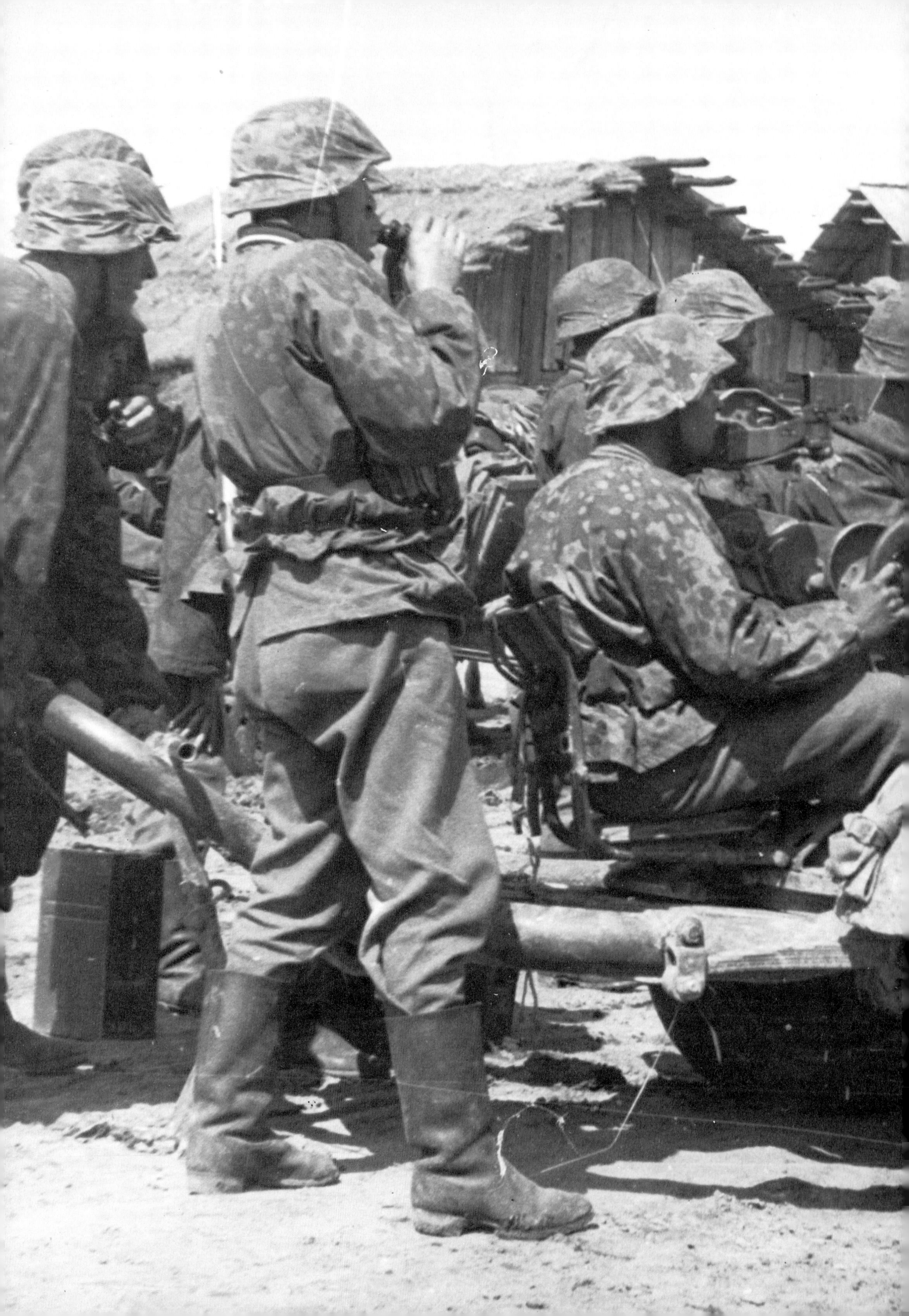

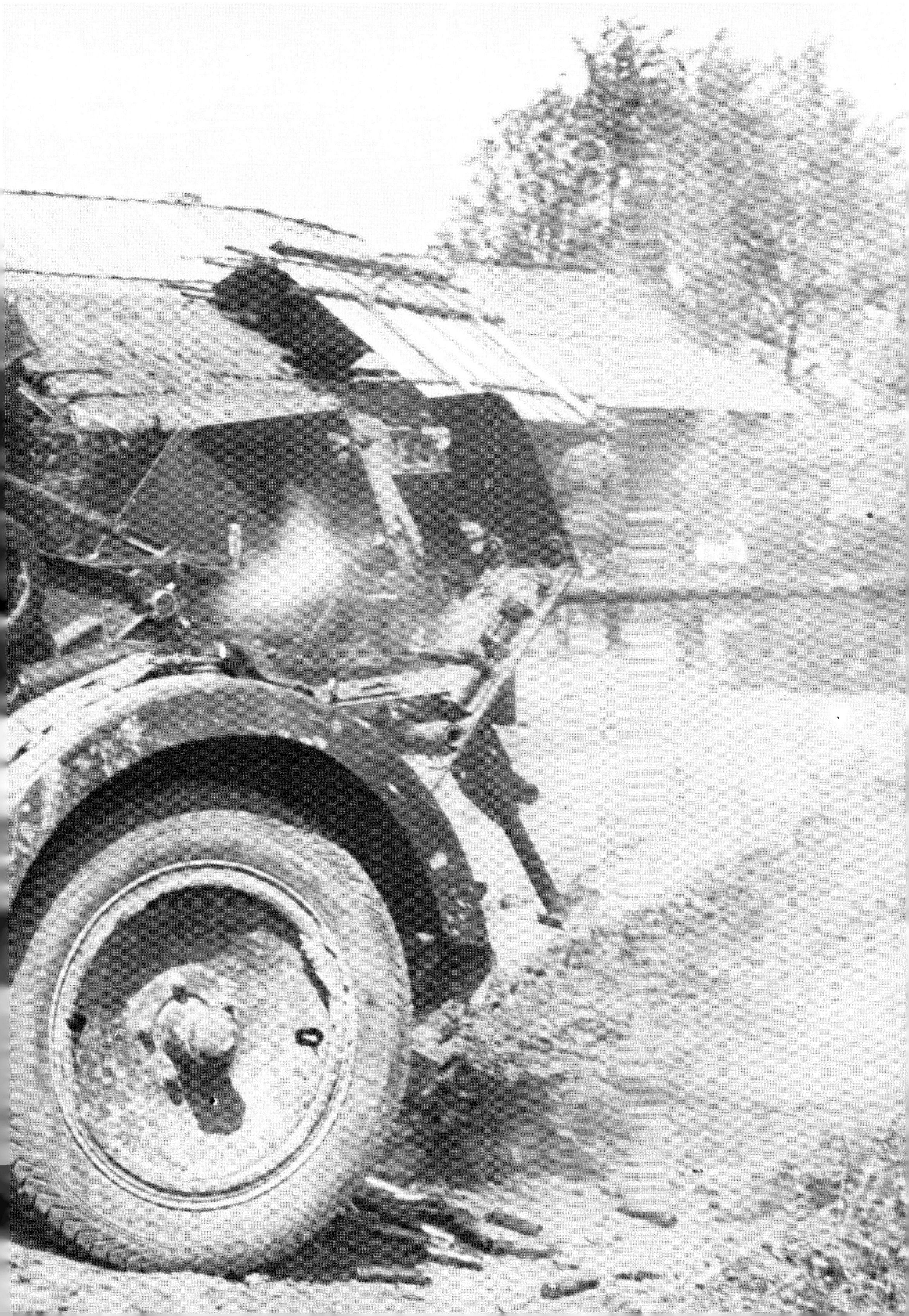

Zivilbevölkerung räumt eine zerstörte Ortschaft.

The civil population leaves a destroyed village.

Die Verfolgung verlangt große Marschleistungen der Grenadiere.

Pursuit demands a high marching performance from the grenadiers.

Das erreichte Angriffsziel wird gesichert.

The objective of the attack is reached and made secure.

Sobald der Gegner sich festsetzt, wird der Vormarsch erneut durch Waffeneinsatz erzwungen, hier 8 cm-Granatwerfer.

Whenever the enemy settles down, weapons are used to force forward the advance, here an 8 cm trench mortar is used.

Durch schwere Brandwunden außer Gefecht gesetzter Unterführer der Waffen-SS wird vom Kameraden liebevoll versorgt.

An Unterführer (NCO) of the Waffen SS who has been incapacitated by severe burn wounds, is caringly looked after by his comrades.

Leichte Feldhaubitze mit Tarnnetz. Das Tornisterfunkgerät überbrückte 5 km.

A light field howitzer with camouflage net. The portable radio equipment has a 5 kilometre range.

„Graupensuppe mit Lorbeerblatt
und Kartoffelstückchen" —

„Barley broth with bay leaves and potato pieces" —

so spiegelt sich der Speiseplan
auf den Gesichtern der Kradschützen wider.

the menu is reflected in the faces of the motorcycle soldiers.

Transportflugzeuge
über dem Einsatzraum
der Division,
die oft aus der Luft versorgt wurde.

Supply planes over the operational area
of the division
which was often provisioned from the air.

Wie oft
begegneten wir
solchen Charakterköpfen
der alten Männer.

How often we met
such characters
among the old men.

Russische Landschaft.

Russian countryside.

Zivilbevölkerung verläßt
die Kampfzone — zugleich
deutsche Kolonne auf
schwierigem Vormarsch
auf Sandwegen.

The civilian population leave
the battle area — at the same
time German columns march
forward with difficulty along
sandy roads.

Abwurfstellen und Landekreuze zeigen den Transport-Ju's die Division „Das Reich".

Dropping zones and landing crosses show the transport Junkers where the „Das Reich" is.

Noch war Sommer.
Was uns bevorstand,
ahnten wir nicht;
es war gut so.
(10,5 cm Haubitze
in Feuerstellung)

It was still summer.
We had no clue
of what lay before us;
this was a good thing.
(10,5 cm howitzer
in its firing position)

Nitschewo — für *sie* ist der Krieg aus,   Nitchevo — for *them* the war is over,

für *uns beginnt er* erst richtig.   Die ersten T34 sind da.

for *us it has only really begun.*   The first T34 are here.

Russischer verwundeter Offizier wird verbunden.

A wounded Russian officer is bandaged.

Schnell voran — auf allen Wegen und behelfsmäßigen Stegen
Forwards fast — by all routes and makeshift ways

unsere Grenadiere.
our grenadiers.

Vernichtete schwere Panzer des Typs T 34.

Heavy tanks of the type T 34, destroyed.

Russischer Bomber notgelandet vor Feldgräbern eines Soldaten der 10. Panzerdivision und des SS-Oberscharführers Göhringer vom Regiment „Deutschland".

An emergency landing by a Russian bomber in front of the battlefield graves of a soldier of the 10th Panzerdivision and of SS Oberscharführer Göhringer of Regiment „Deutschland".

Spähwagenbesatzung schickt Gefangene „nach hinten".

The crew of a reconnaissance car send prisoners „to the rear".

Feind von links!

The enemy is on the left!

Die Kompanien der Grenadierregimenter waren noch nicht dezimiert
und 1941 jeder Aufgabe im Angriff wie in der Verteidigung voll gewachsen.
Sie *waren* . . .

The companies of the grenadier regiments were not yet decimated
and by 1941 were equal to every task both on the offensive and in defence.
That is how they *were* . . .

Mitte Juli ein aufschlußreicher Wald von Wegweisern.

A comprehensive collection of signposts, in mid July.

Verlassene russische Feldbefestigungen, die oft noch von versteckten Gegnern besetzt waren, deren „Besichtigung" oft genug deutschen Soldaten zum Verhängnis wurde.

Abandoned Russian field positions which were often still occupied by hidden enemy soldiers. „Visiting" them often enough proved fatal for the German soldiers.

Zerschlagener russischer Feldflugplatz.

A destroyed Russian operational airfield.

Der neu auftretende russische Panzer
T 34 war ein „Problem".
Seine Schnelligkeit, Panzerung
und Bewaffnung machte ihn
sehr gefährlich.
3,7 cm Pak überwalzt.

The newly introduced Russian tank T 34
was a „problem". Its speed, armour
and armament made it very dangerous.
A knocked-out 3,7 cm Pak.

Erst eine leichte Feldhaubitze
vernichtete ihn
auf 5 m Entfernung

It took a light field howitzer
at a distance of 5 metres to destroy it

und schoß ihn in Brand.

and shoot it up in flames.

Dem Kampfeseifer der Grenadiere waren die ersten Erfolge mit zuzuschreiben.

The first successes resulted in the eagerness of fighting.

Der ehemalige Chef der 8. Kompanie berichtet zu den Bildern der Seite 118:

The former head of the 8th Company made a report to the photographs shown on page 118:

„Das II. Bataillon des 11. Regiments war ostwärts Jelnja, nordostwärts Jeremina eingesetzt. Hinter dem Batl. war die Feuerstellung der 6. Batterie des Artillerieregimentes „Das Reich". Plötzlich bewegten sich 5 schwere Feindpanzer in Richtung der eigenen Hauptkampflinie. Zwei drehten ab, drei rollten unaufhaltsam weiter. Eine 3,7 cm Pak hinter der HKL wurde niedergewalzt. Eine leichte Feldhaubitze wurde im Mannschaftszug hinter eine kleine Kuppe gebracht. Auf 15 m Entfernung nahm das Geschütz den Kampf mit dem Panzer auf. Durch einen Treffer auf den Turmkranz fing der Panzer Feuer und kam 5 m vor dem Geschütz zum Stillstand. Ich erlebte diesen Feuerkampf aus wenigen Metern Entfernung und wurde dabei verwundet. Damals war ich Chef der 8./Rgt. 11. (Wisliceny)

The II Battalion of the 11th Regiment was sent into action east of Jelnja and north-east of Jeremina. To the rear of the Battalion was the firing position of the 6th Battery of the Artillery Regiment „Das Reich". Suddenly five heavy tanks of the enemy moved in the direction of our own front line. Two turned off, three rolled inexorably onwards. A 3,7 cm Pak behind the front line was crushed into the ground. A light field howitzer was dragged by its crew behind a small rise in the ground. At a distance of 15 metres, the gun took up the fight with the tank. The tank caught fire from a direct hit on its turret ring and came to a halt 5 metres in front of the gun. I experienced this exchange of fire from a few metres distance and was wounded as a result of it. At the time I was commander of 8th/Regt. 11. (Wisliceny)"

SS-Gruppenführer
u. Generalleutnant
der Waffen-SS
Paul Hausser,
Divisionskommandeur

SS-Oberführer Hansen,
Kommandeur
des Artillerie-Regimentes

SS-Sturmbannführer Kumm,
Kommandeur des Infanterie-Regiments
„Der Führer"

SS-Hauptsturmführer
Fritz Klingenberg,
Kommandeur
d. Kradschützen-Btl.

SS-Sturmbannführer Weiß,
Kommandeur
der Nachrichten-Abteilung

Fliegerverbindungs
d. Luftwaffe (Flivo

...sturmführer
...lenkamp,
...ndeur
...lärungsabteilung

SS-Hauptsturmführer Landwehr,
Kommandeur
Panzerjäger-Abteilung

SS-Sturmbannführer Raddatz,
Waffen- u. Munitionsoffizier (Wa Mun)
Quartiermeister-Abteilung
d. Division

SS-Untersturmführer Mix
3. Generalstabsoffizier (Ic)

Divisionsgefechtsstand Raum Smolensk.
Lagebesprechung vor dem Angriff auf den Kessel von Kiew.

Divisional HQ near Smolensk.
Briefing before attacking the Kiev Cauldron.

Beobachtung
durch das
Scherenfernrohr.

Observation
through the scissors periscope.

Kameradengrab am Wegesrand bei Jelnja.
A battlefield-grave of comrades besides a road near Jelnja.

Der Vormarsch auf Jelnja 15. Juli wird fortgesetzt — 298 km bis Moskau —
dann Ende Juli härtester Widerstand.

The advance on Jelnja is renewed on 15th July — 298 kms to Moscow —
then at the end of July, very tough resistance.

Regiment „Der Führer" bei Koloschina ostwärts Jelnja.

Regiment „Der Führer" at Koloschina, east of Jelnja.

Granatwerfer in Feuerstellung im Jelnja-Bogen, Juli 1941.

Trench-mortar in firing position at Jelnja salient, July 1941.

Schwere Artillerie des „Iwan"
bedrängt uns
am schwerumkämpften
Jelnjabogen.

„Ivan's" heavy artillery
oppresses us in the heavily contested
Jelnja salient.

Selbst in der Stellung
herrscht Ordnung.

Even in a field position,
orderliness prevails.

Kradmelder.

A despatch-rider.

Im Kampf genommene Stellung der Russen.

A Russian position captured in battle.

Russischer Divisionskommandeur vom III./SS-„DF" gefangengenommen.

A Russian divisional commander captured by III SS „DF".

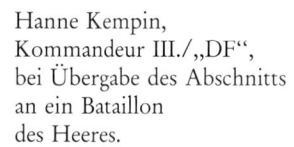

Hanne Kempin, Kommandeur III./„DF", bei Übergabe des Abschnitts an ein Bataillon des Heeres.

Hanne Kempin, commander of III „DF", handing over of the sector to a battalion of the army.

Pause auf einem Gefechtsstand bei Jelnja August 1941.   A break at a command post at Jelnja August 1941.

Oberscharführer Friedl vor Jelnja.

Oberscharführer Friedl before Jelnja.

Meldeblock auf den Knien,
Erkennungsmarke umgehängt,
tief im Erdloch.
Der Blitzkrieg ist zu Ende.
Die Heeresgruppe Mitte
liegt fest.

Message pad on his knees,
identification tag hanging around
his neck, deep in a dugout.
The „Blitzkrieg" is over.
The Army Group Centre
is immobilized.

Kameraden des Heeres
werden von einem Unterführer
der Waffen-SS eingewiesen.

Army (Heer) comrades are briefed by an
Unterführer of the Waffen SS.

Pioniere
mit elektrischem
Minensuchgerät.

Pioneers with an electrical
mine detector.

Für eine Behelfsbrücke
schneiden sich die Pioniere
die Kanthölzer mit Kraftsäge zu.

Pioneers cut wooden sections
with a power saw for an emergency bridge.

Panzer-Späher bei Chominskij
(4.9.41 Martin/Hahn).

An armoured reconnaissance car at Chaminsky
(4.9.41 Martin/Hahn).

Der für sein Land kämpfende russische Soldat war von großer Standfestigkeit

The Russian soldier fighting for his country stood firm with great resolution

und unsere Verluste überstiegen alle Befürchtungen.

and our losses exceeded all our fears.

Am 6.9.41 bei der Schließung des Kessels von Kiew nach hartem Kampf um Makoschin und Priluki.

On 6.9.41 during the closing of the Kiev Cauldron after hard fighting around Makoschin and Priluki.

Der Panzerzug
von Makoschin
von Stukas zerstört,
nachdem „Das Reich"
ihn durch Schienen-
sprengung gestellt
hatte.

The armoured train
from Makoschin
destroyed by dive bombers
after „Das Reich"
had immobilized it
by blowing up the tracks.

Hauptsturmführer Stadler mit 5. Kompanie des Regiments „DF" mit Unterstützung durch Sturmgeschütze am 16.9.41 bei Priluki.

Hauptsturmführer Stadler with 5th Company of the Regiment „DF", supported by an assault gun, on 16.9.41 at Priluki.

Gefechtsstand Regiment „DF";
links SS-Sturmbannführer Kumm und SS-Brigadeführer und Generalmajor der Waffen-SS Keppler.

Regiment „DF" command;
on the left, SS Sturmbannführer Kumm and SS Brigadeführer and Major General of the Waffen SS Keppler.

Bereitstellung des XXXXVI. Korps mit 10. Panzerdivision und Division „Das Reich".

XXXXVI Corps with 10th Panzer Division and Division „Das Reich" form up.

Schweres Maschinengewehr unterstützt den Angriff der Grenadiere.   A heavy machine-gun supports the grenadiers' attack.

Ordnung muß bleiben.
Orderliness is a necessity.

Straßenbau.
Road-construction.

Nur wer todmüde ist, schläft auch in dieser Lage im Kübelwagen.

Only someone who is dead tired, sleeps in this position in the Kübelwagen (jeep).

Briefe der Panzerjäger in die Heimat.

Letters home from the anti-tank soldiers.

Gefechtsstand in einer russischen Balka (Schlucht).

Command post in a Russian balka (gorge).

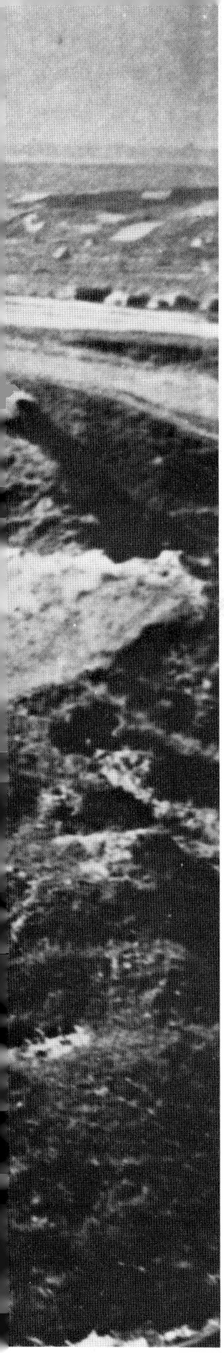
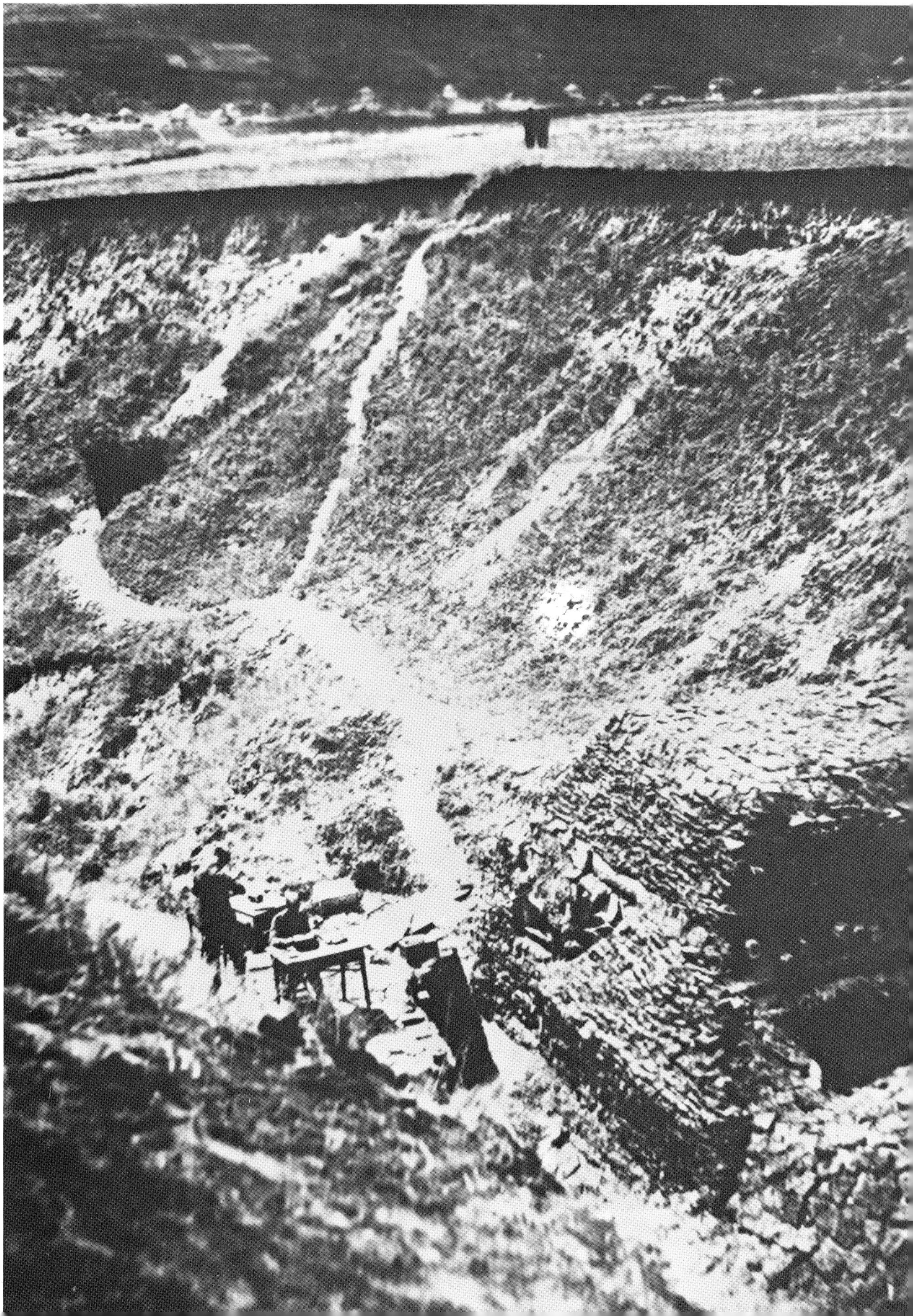

Noch während des Brückenbaus setzen Kradschützen bereits über — Schnelligkeit ist eine „Waffe" —
der Gegner soll sich nicht wieder festsetzen — das spart Blut.

Motor-cycle infantry cross over while the bridge is still being built — speed is a „weapon" —
the enemy must not be allowed to settle down again — this saves blood.

Wenige Tage nach Jelnja halfen unsere Männer den Russen ein paar Tage bei der Ernte — kaum zu glauben!

A day or so after Jelnja our men helped the Russians for a few days with the harvest — hardly credible!

Der Ia der Division, Werner Ostendorff (gefallen 1945), mit Heinz Harmel, Kdr. II./DF und Hans Lingner, Kdr. III./DF bei einer Rücksprache.

The Senior Staff of the Division, Werner Ostendorff (killed in action 1945), with Heinz Harmel, commander of II „DF" and Hans Lingner, commander of III „DF" in conference.

Auf dem Weg zur Schließung des Kessels von Kiew.   On the way to closing the Kiev Cauldron.

3,7 cm Pak
in Lauerstellung.

3,7 cm Pak
in an ambush position.

Über die Brücke von Makoschin, die vorher von eigenen Sturmkampffliegern versehentlich angegriffen wird und hohe eigene Verluste kostet.

Over Makoschin bridge, which a little time before was attacked by mistake by own fighter bombers causing us great losses.

Kameradenhilfe.

Comradely assistance.

Der 3. Generalstabsoffizier (Ic) vernimmt einen russischen Offizier.

The third general staff officer (Ic) interrogates a Russian officer.

Eine schwere Gruppe macht sich zum weiteren Angriff fertig. SS-Hauptscharführer Blauensteiner bei Priluki 16.9.1941.

A group with heavy weapons makes ready for a further attack. SS Hauptscharführer Blauensteiner at Priluki 16.9.1941.

Ein kampfstarker Stoßtrupp hat russische Panzersoldaten als Gefangene eingebracht, deren Vernehmung der Aufklärung dient und ständig notwendig ist.

An assault group of combat strength has brought in Russian tank soldiers as prisoners, the interrogation of whom serves intelligence and is constantly necessary.

Provisorische Gefangenensammelstellen —
Kampftruppen gaben die gegnerischen Soldaten schnell ab (Sturmmann Löbl, 7./„DF").

A provisional collecting point for prisoners —
the fighting troops quickly handed over the enemy soldiers (Sturmmann Löbl of the 7th „DF").

Erbeutete Waffen.
Captured weapons.

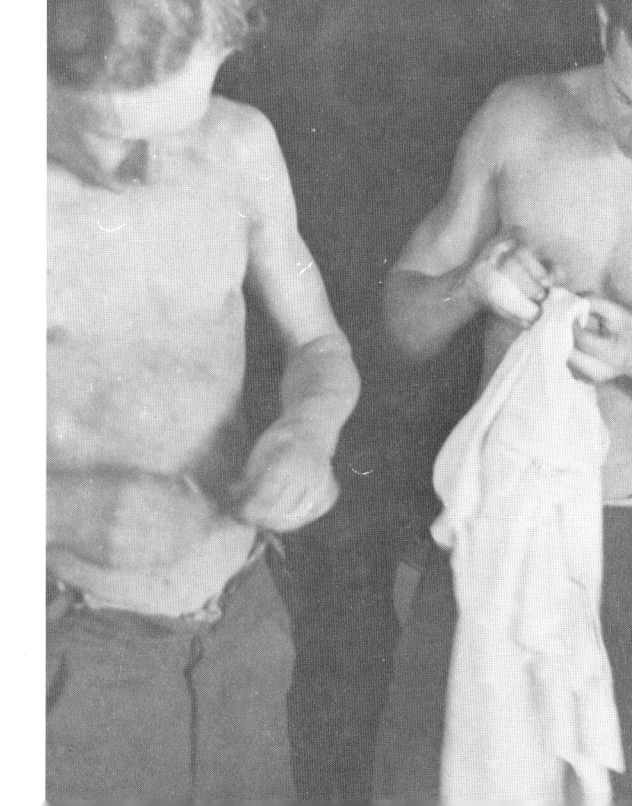

Quälgeister werden gesammelt.
Collecting the tormentors.

Die Zeit des Vorwärtsstürmens ist vorbei.
In die Erde — auseinander — das ist nötig.

The time for storming is past.
They go to ground —
spaced out from one another —
which is necessary.

Unser „Bungalow".

Our „bungalow".

Stabswanze müßte man sein.

A comfortable job at the rear is what we would all like.

Bei uns ist's gemütlich.

It is cosy here with us.

Es ist
schon kalt
in der Frühe.

It's cold
in the
early morning.

Herbst 1941.
Autumn 1941.

146

Sturmgeschütze und Kradschützen.
Assault guns and motorcycle infantry.

Der Divisionskommandeur, SS-Gruppenführer und Generalleutnant der Waffen-SS Paul Hausser, damals 61 Jahre alt, wird von SS-Hauptsturmführer Klingenberg vor dem Angriff auf Moskau in die Lage eingewiesen.

The divisional commander, SS Gruppenführer und Lieutenant-General of the Waffen SS Paul Hausser, then 61 years old, is briefed about the situation by SS Hauptsturmführer Klingenberg before the attack on Moscow.

Oberbefehlshaber der Panzergruppe 2,
Generaloberst Heinz Guderian,
dem die Division „Das Reich" unterstand.

Commander-in-Chief of Panzer Group 2, Colonel General Heinz Guderian,
under whose command was the Division „Das Reich".

Kommandeur der Division „Das Reich"
bis zu seiner Verwundung am 14.10.41 vor Jelnja,
SS-Gruppenführer und Generalleutnant der Waffen-SS
Paul Hausser, hier im Gespräch mit dem Kommandierenden
General des XXXXVI. Panzerkorps, General der Panzertruppen
von Vietinghoff-Scheel.

Commander of the Division „Das Reich"
until he was wounded outside Jelnja on 14.10.41,
SS Gruppenführer und Lieutenant General of the Waffen SS Paul Hausser,
here speaking with the General commanding the XXXXVI Panzer Corps,
General of the Panzertroops von Vietinghoff-Scheel.

Nachfolger als Kommandeur „Das Reich" wurde
SS-Brigadeführer und Generalmajor der Waffen-SS
Wilhelm Bittrich.

Sucessor as commander of „Das Reich" was SS Brigadeführer
and Major General of the Waffen SS Wilhelm Bittrich.

Am 14.10.41 wurde Hausser hier schwer verwundet (Verlust eines Auges).

On 14.10.41, Hausser was severely wounded here (loss of one eye).

Die Moskauer Schutzstellung ist mit den Panzern der 10. Panzerdivision durchbrochen.

Panzers of the 10th Panzer Division break through the defensive positions of Moscow.

Schlamm und Brei
behindern Operationen
und vor allem den Nachschub.

Mud and slush hamper
operations especially
the bringing up of supplies.

150

Die 10. Panzerdivision des Heeres,
die 2. SS-Division „Das Reich" und
das Regiment „Großdeutschland"
bilden das Korps.

The 10th Panzer Division of the Army
(Heer), the 2nd SS Division „Das Reich"
and the Regiment „Großdeutschland"
forme the Corps.

Vormarschstraße westlich Moskau — Unsagbar schwer der Vormarsch.
Line of advance west of Moscow — The advance was unspeakably hard.

Menschen und Tiere
erdulden des Winters Gewalt.

Men and animals
suffer under the terrible winter.

Divisionszeichen am Mast in Gshatsk.

Divisional sign at a pole in Gshatsk.

Offenes Feuer unter dem Motor
zur Erwärmung des Motorenöls,
sonst lief nichts mehr.
Lkw des Artillerie-Regiments 7. Nov. 1941 bei Rusa
(Knüppeldamm, siehe Karte Seite 182 „Division Das Reich"
Band III).

An open fire under the engine to warm the motor oil,
otherwise nothing would run any more.
A heavy truck of the Artillery Regiment on 7th November 1941
at Rusa (Knüppeldamm, see map on page 182
„Division Das Reich" Volume III).

Bei 20 ° unter Null im Freien.

20 ° C below zero out in the open.

Alle Fugen
abdichten gegen
Wärmeverlust.

Block up gaps
against heat loss.

Zehn Kilometer südlich Gshatsk
abgeschossenes Kfz.

A shot up vehicle
ten kilometres south of Gshatsk.

Bei Istra, 70 km westlich Moskau, traf die Division auf frische sibirische Gardetruppen der Fernostarmee. „Die Sibirier mußten weichen" (Carell in „Barbarossa").

Near Istra, 70 kilometres west of Moscow, the division came across fresh Siberian Guard troops of the Far East Army. „The Siberians had to give ground" (Carell in „Barbarossa").

Nur 25 km bis zum Roten Platz in Moskau.
Only 25 kilometres to Red Square in Moscow.

Längst hatte sich die Truppe Ende Dezember 1941 Schlitten beschafft, um beweglich zu bleiben.

By the end of December 1941, the troops had long since got hold of sledges, in order to maintain their mobility.

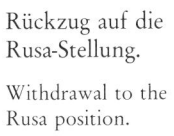

Rückzug auf die Rusa-Stellung.

Withdrawal to the Rusa position.

Anfang Januar 1942 übernimmt SS-Brigadeführer und Generalmajor der Waffen-SS Kleinheisterkamp (gefallen 1945) die Division und führt sie in der Winterschlacht von Sytschewka bei größter Kälte. Unser Bild wurde bei Sytschewka aufgenommen.

At the beginning of January 1942, SS Brigadeführer and Major General of the Waffen SS Kleinheisterkamp (killed in action 1945) took over command of the division and led it during the winter battle of Sytschewka in conditions of extreme cold. Our picture was taken near Sytschewka.

Grenadier der Waffen-SS Januar 1942.

Grenadier of the Waffen SS in January 1942.

Wachsam bleiben.   Continuous vigilance.

Winterbekleidung endlich da.   Winter clothing has at last arrived.

Nachts 52 ° Frost — am Tage 30 ° und Sonnenschein Januar 1942.   52 ° C of frost at night. Sunshine and 30 ° Centigrade below zero by day in January 1942

Das SS-Regiment „Der Führer"
wird an der Wolga
durch Generaloberst Model
nach Durchbruch der
29. sowjetischen Armee
bei 40 ° in die Lücke geworfen.
Befehl: „Unter allen Umständen
halten", lautet Models
persönlicher Befehl an Kumm.
„Unter allen Umständen",
wiederholte der General
noch einmal mit Nachdruck.
Kumm grüßte:
„Jawohl, Herr General!"

At minus 40 ° the SS Regiment
„Der Führer" is thrown into the gap
by Colonel-General Model on the Volga
after the break-through of the
29th Soviet Army.
Order: „Hold under all
circumstances" read Model's
personal order to Kumm.
„Under all circumstances."
repeated the general with emphasis.
Kumm saluted.
„It will be done, Herr General."

Generaloberst Model, Oberbefehlshaber der 9. Armee,
im Gespräch mit SS-Standartenführer Ostendorff.

Colonel-General Model, Commander-in-Chief of the 9th Army,
talking with SS Standartenführer Ostendorff.

Das MG ist mit Schneebrett
standsicherer geworden.
Die Truppe wußte sich zu helfen.

The light M-G is made more stable
with snow boards.
The troops knew how to help themselves.

Nördlich Sytschewka Ende Januar 1942 2 cm Flak im Mannschaftszug.

North of Sytschewka at the end of January 1942, a 2 cm Flak towed by men.

Am 20. Januar 1942 wird der Rest des Rgts. „Deutschland" mit der Bahn verladen und in den Bereitstellungsraum nach Bogdanowo geführt.

On 20th January 1942 the rest of the Regiment „Deutschland" entrains and travels to Bogdanowo to the assembly area.

Nördlich Sytschewka Januar 1942 in vorderster Linie.

North of Sytschewka January 1942, up at the front line.

An der Bahnlinie nach Rshew Gegenstoß mit Sturmgeschütz der 1. Panzerdivision auf Borodino.

The railway line to Rshew — counter-attack with assault gun of the 1st Panzer Division towards Borodino.

Nördlich Sytschewka am 21. Januar 1942.   North of Sytschewka on 21st January 1942.

Nördlich Sytschewka mit Teilen der 1. Panzerdivision.
Feinddruchbruch westlich Rshew.
Die Heeresgruppe kämpft um das Überleben.

North of Sytschewka with parts of the 1st Panzer Division.
Enemy break-through west of Rshew.
The Army Group fights for survival.

Das Regiment „DF" wird mit 2 Bataillonen mit 650 Mann zum Sondereinsatz zum AOK 9 (Model) abgegeben.

The Regiment „DF" with two battalions of 650 men, is seconded to AOK 9 (Model) for a special assignment.

Infanterie Kampfgruppe
bei Rshew Februar 1942.

Infantry combat group
at Rshew in February 1942.

→

Bild folgender
Seiten 168/169:
Otto Kumm,
Kommandeur
4. Rgt. „DF"
verleiht
Eiserne Kreuze

Photograph
pages 168/169:
Otto Kumm,
CO 4 Rgt. „DF"
awards
Iron Crosses.

Wolga-Stellung
westlich Rshew.

A position on the Volga
west of Rshew.

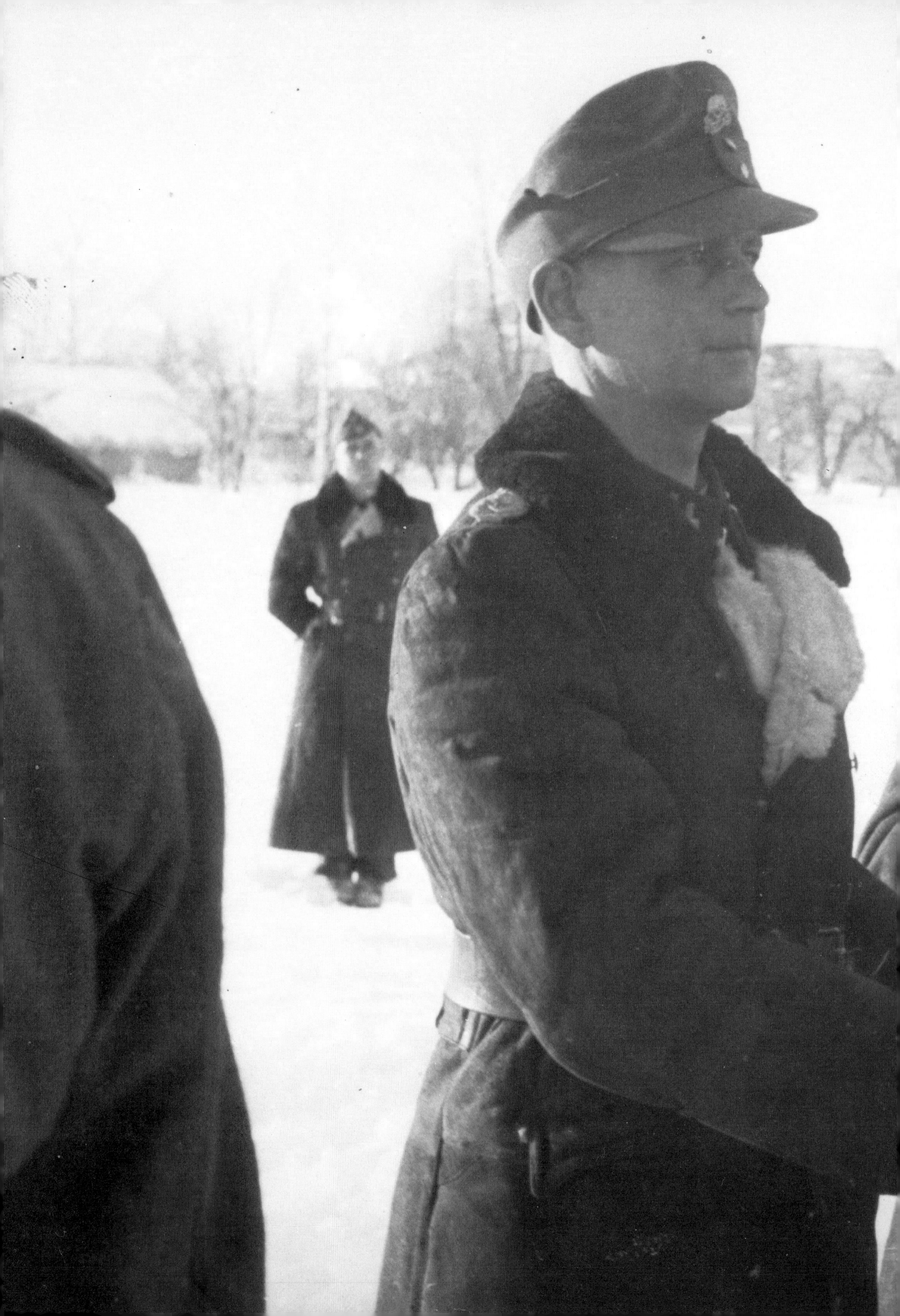

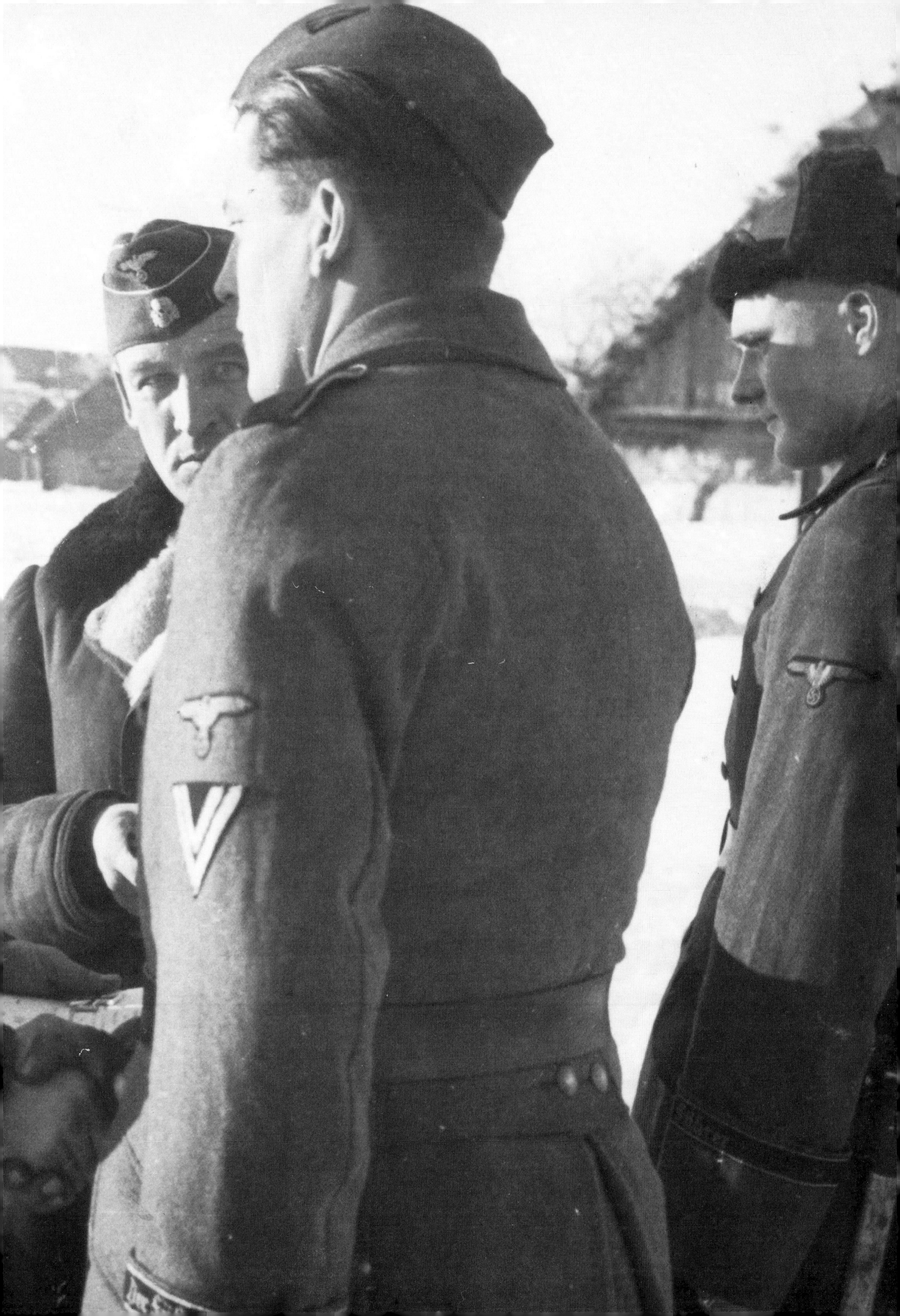

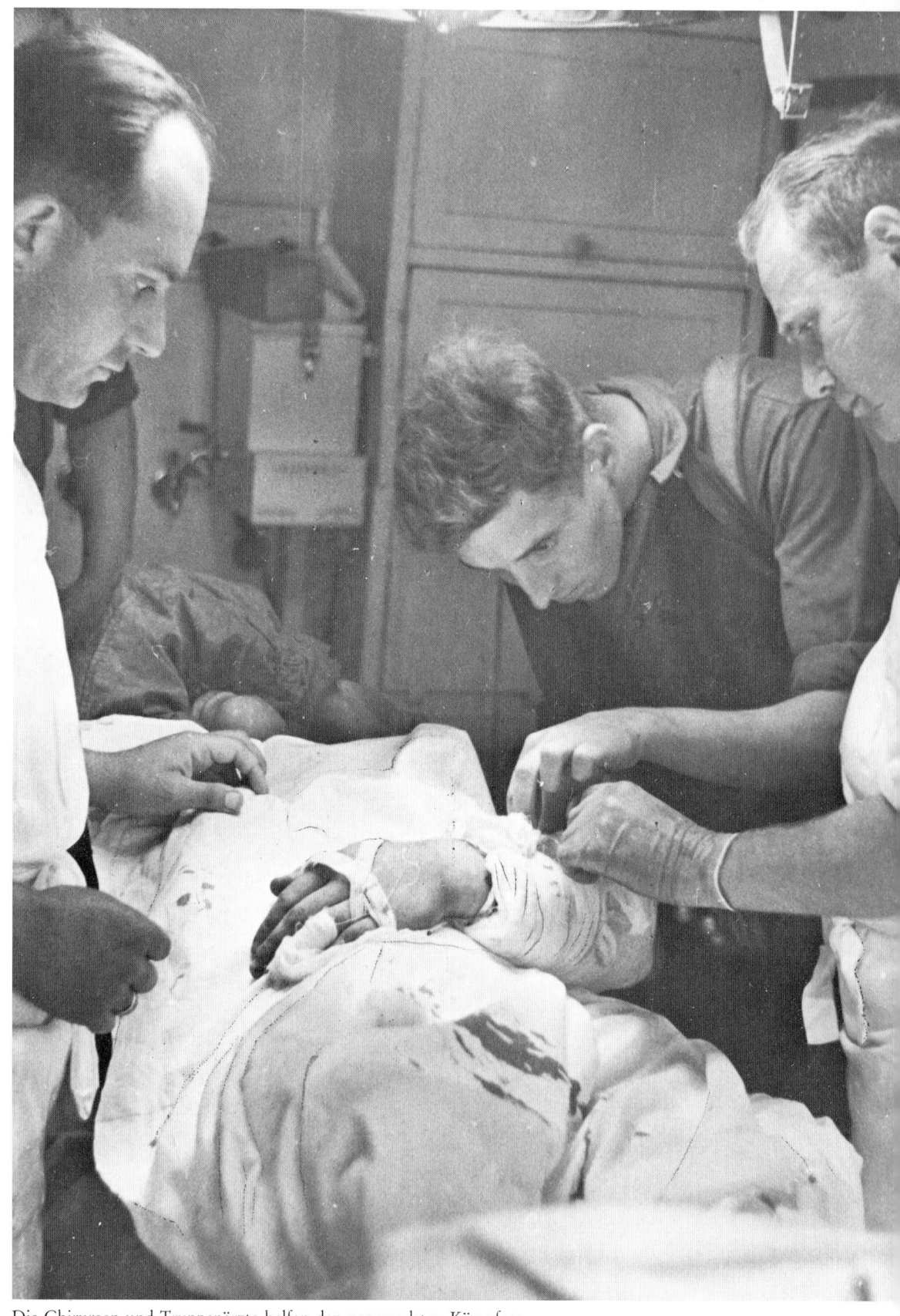

Die Chirurgen und Truppenärzte helfen den verwundeten Kämpfern.

The surgeons and medical officers help the wounded combatants.

Die 3,7 cm Pak war fast unbrauchbar, aber die Truppe hatte nichts anderes.
Sie wurde auf Schlittenkufen für den Winter beweglich gemacht. Die *Division* war nur noch eine Kampfgruppe.

The 3,7 cm Pak was almost unusable, but the troops did not have anything else.
It was put on sledge runners to make it mobile in winter. The *Division* was by now only a battle group.

Der Nachschub in der trostlosen Schneewüste Mittelrußlands auf russischen Panjeschlitten Ende Februar 1942 by Rshew.

Supplies on Russian panje sledges in the desolate snow desert of central Russia near Rshew in February 1942.

Vorbei an der russischen 7,62 cm (Ratsch-Bum) auf Spähtrupp.

Past a Russion 7,62 cm („Ratsch-Bum" was its onomatopoeic nick name) on reconnaissance.

Posten beim Kompanie-Gefechtsstand März 1942.

Sentries at the company command post in March 1942.

Soldaten sind nie Nutznießer der Kriege.
Diese im „Hantelwald" März 1942 schon gar nicht.

Soldiers are never the profiteers of war.
Especially not these ones in „Dumb Bell Wood" in March 1942.

Vor dem „Stiefelwald"
im Abschnitt Rshew
März 1942
bei den Männern
des Regiments
„Deutschland".

In front of „Boot Wood"
in the Rshew sector in
March 1942, with men
of the Regiment
„Deutschland".

Rgts.-Gefechtsstand SS-„Deutschland" in der Wolgastellung westlich Rshew bei Petunowo nach Artillerieüberfall.

The battle H.Q. of the SS Regiment „Deutschland" in the Volga position west of Rshew at Petunowo after artillery fire.

Pak 5 cm (38) westlich Rshew in der Wolgastellung.

5 cm Pak (38) west of Rshew in the Volga position.

Ablösung der Kampfgruppe „Reich" (Hantelwald).

The battle group „Reich" is relieved (Dumb Bell Wood).

Schi-Kompanie SS-„Deutschland".

Ski company SS „Deutschland".

174 Verlegung mit Eisenbahntransport.   Redeployment by rail transport.

Im Schneesturm vor.

Forward in a snow storm.

Männer vom Regiment „DF".
Improvisierte Wintertarnbekleidung.

Men of the Regiment „DF".
Improvised winter camouflage clothing.

Härteste Kämpfe im „Birkenwäldchen" — zusammengetragene Gefallene des tapfer kämpfenden Feindes.

Very hard fighting in „Little Birch Wood" — the dead of the enemy who fought courageously, gathered together.

Spähtrupp im Keulenwald.

A reconnaissance patrol in „Club Wood".

Auf geht's!

Lets go!

Sichernder MG-Schütze.

An machine-gunner gives cover.

Bei Dorogino am 13.3.42
bricht die Sonne durch das Gewölk.
Zur Nachtzeit herrschen noch 40 °.

On 13.3.42 at Dorogino, the sun breaks
through the clouds. In the night time,
minus 40 ° is still the rule.

Im Keulenwald sind die Reste
der Division bespannt
und nicht mehr motorisiert.

In „Club Wood" the rest of the division
is horse-drawn and no longer motorized.

Feldpost-Ausgabe.

Field post distribution.

März 1942
und erste Marketenderware.

March 1942
and the first canteen supplies.

Stellung I. Bataillon des Regimentes „Deutschland" im „Hantelwald" ostwärts Panowo am 20. März 1942.

Positions of the 1st Battalion of the Regiment „Deutschland" in „Dumb Bell Wood" east of Panowo on 20th March 1942.

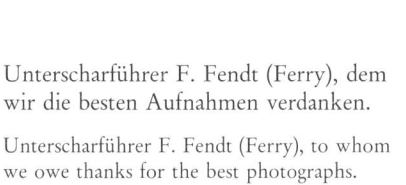

Unterscharführer F. Fendt (Ferry), dem wir die besten Aufnahmen verdanken.

Unterscharführer F. Fendt (Ferry), to whom we owe thanks for the best photographs.

Was Front-soldaten brauchen.

What front line soldiers need.

181

Rottenführer Wlassak
bei der Entlausung
im „Keulenwald"
(Stabskompanie Regiment „Deutschland")

Rottenführer Wlassak
during delousing in „Club Wood"
(Staff company of the Regiment „Deutschland").

Eisenbahnmarsch.
Railway transport.

Sie konnten
sich auf kameradschaftliche
Hilfe absolut verlassen,
sie bleibt Grundelement
auch heute.

They could rely upon
the help of their comrades,
this remained a fundamental
element even today.

Schwerverwundete
werden geborgen
und versorgt.

Serously wounded
were recovered
and dressed.

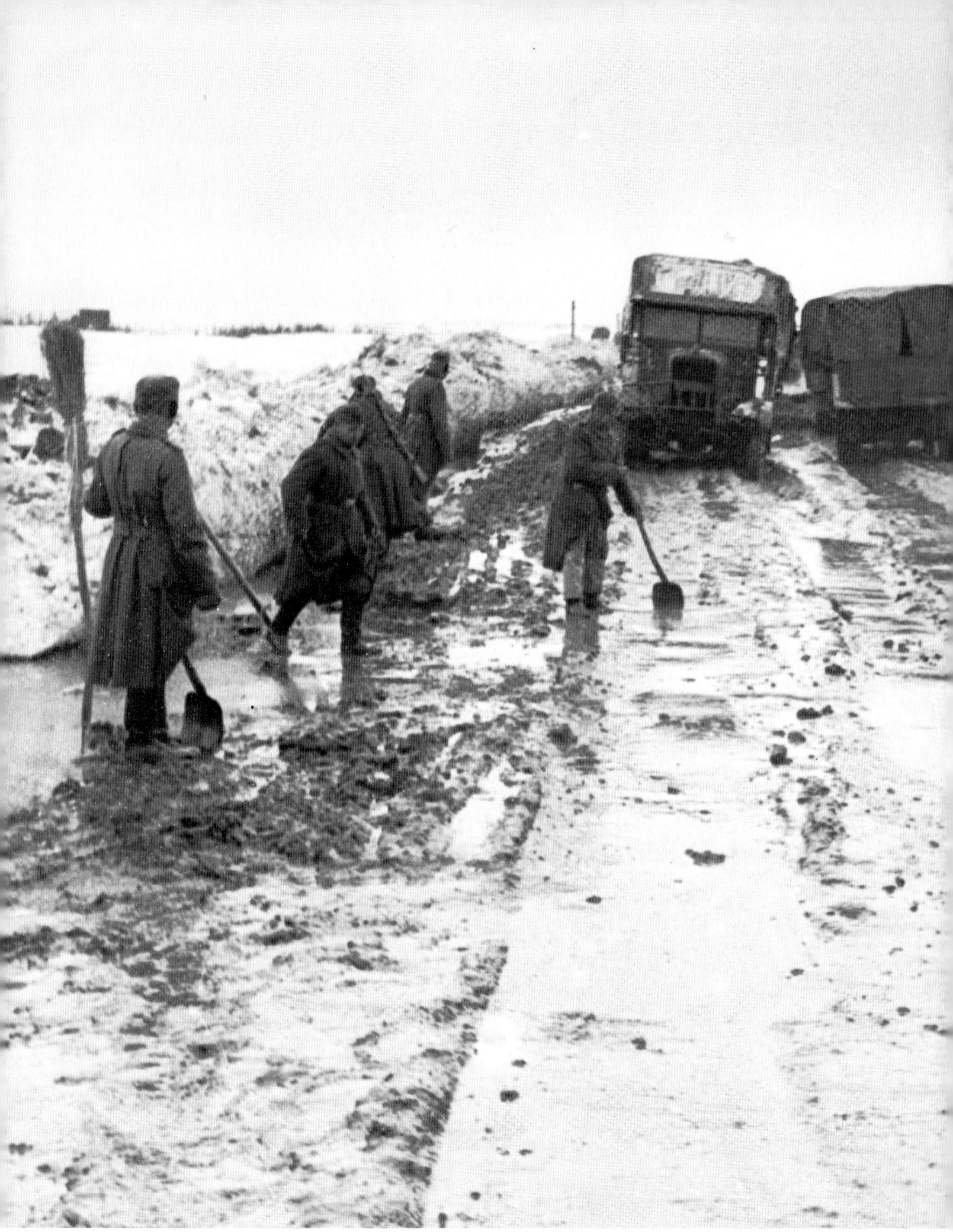

Der schlimme Winter weicht dem Frühling.

The terrible winter gives way to the spring.

Verlegung nach Frankreich zur Neuaufstellung als Panzergrenadierdivision.

Transfer to France for new formation and conversion into a panzer grenadier division.

Die Reste der Division kommen nach Frankreich und in das Heimatkriegsgebiet zur Neuaufstellung und Umgliederung zu einer Panzergrenadier-Division.

The remains of the division come back to France and the home front region to be reorganized and reformed as a panzer grenadier division.

5 cm Panzerabwehrkanone im motorisierten Zug mit 1 ½ Tonnen Halbkettenfahrzeug.

Motorized tow of a 5 cm anti-tank gun with a 1 ½ ton half-track vehicle.

Panzergrenadiere bei Übungen in Montmartin (Frankreich).

Panzer grenadiers on exercise in Montmartin (France).

Eine Panzerabteilung kommt dazu.

A panzer Battalion is added.

Panzer IV mit 7,5 cm Kanone.
Panzer IV with a 7,5 cm gun.

Fernsprechtrupp bei der Leitungsprobe.
Signals check the lines.

5 cm Pak in Stellung

5 cm Pak in position.

Die Umgliederung
zur Panzergrandier-Division
ist im Gange.
Die neuen schweren Waffen
werden im Herbst 1942
bei Montmartin
in vielen Übungen erprobt.
Der Kommandierende General
besichtigt (Harmel und Hausser).

Reorganisation as a panzer grenadier
division is in progress. The new heavy
weapons are tried out in many exercises
in autumn 1942 in Montmartin.
The General Officer Commanding
makes a visit.

Panzer IV des neuaufgestellten
2. SS-Panzerregiments.
Erst jetzt bekommen wir Panzer.

Panzer IV of the new formed
2nd SS Panzer Regiment.
Only now do we get tanks.

Französischer Schlachtkreuzer „Dunkerque", 26 500 Tonnen Wasserverdrängung, 8 x 33 cm schwere Artillerie in Vierlingstürmen, 16 x 13 cm Mittelartillerie, 21 Seemeilen Geschwindigkeit, Oelfeuerung (Turbinen), 29 000 indiz. Pferdestärke, 166 m lang, 27 m b., 8,9 m tief mit 1131 Mann Besatzung (Schwesterschiff „Straßbourg") sank auf ebenem Kiel.
Das Schwesterschiff wurde im Dock mit diesem geflutet.

French armoured-cruiser „Dunkerque", 26 500 t displacement-tonnage. 8 heavy guns, 33 cm, in four-gun-turrets. 16 medium guns, 13 cm. Velocity 21 nautical miles. Oil-burning (turbines), 29 000 indicated hp. Length 166 m, width 27 m, 3,9 m deep-drawing. Crew 1.131. The twin-ship was the „Strassbourg". The battleship sank on even keel. The twin-ship was grounded at the same tine in the dockyard.

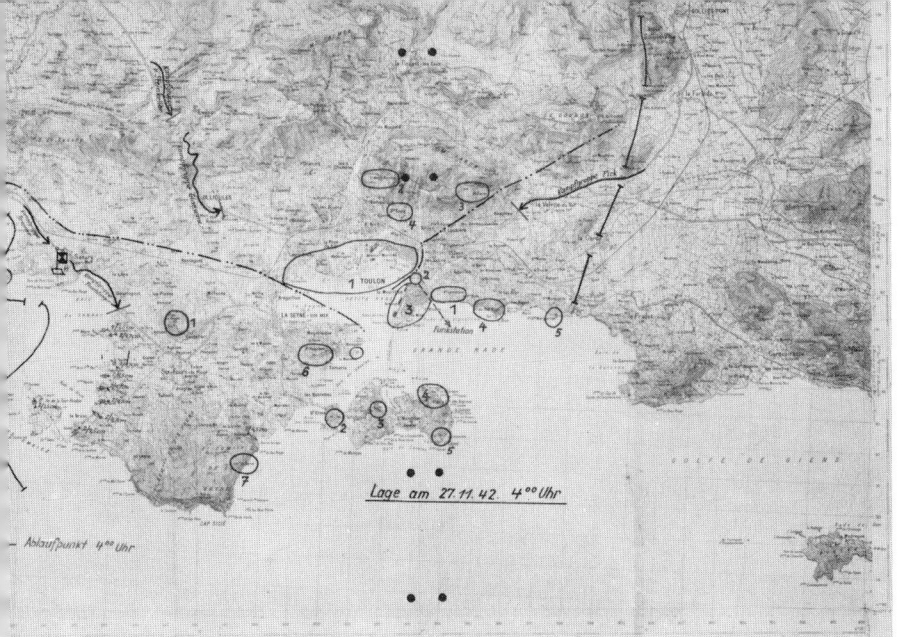

Unternehmen Handstreich Toulon

Operation „coup-de-main" Toulon

Hafen Toulon —
Kampfgruppe „Das Reich"
nordostwärts mit Spitze und
Kampfgruppen 7. Panzerdivision
nordwestlich — mit Luftwaffe und Marine —
beide unter dem Kommando
des SS-Panzerkorps (Hausser)
am 27.11.42 um 4.00 Uhr.

Toulon Harbour —
Battle Group „Das Reich" north-east
with the spear-head and
Battle Group 7th Panzer Division to the north-west
— with the Air Force and Navy —
both under the command of the SS Panzer Corps
(Hausser) on 27-11-42 at 04.00 hours.

In Wahrung der Flaggenehre versenkt der französische Admiral de Laborde fast die gesamte Flotte, über die Frankreich noch verfügt. Dreiundsiebzig Einheiten sinken, sieben Admirale und 27 000 Marinesoldaten werden gefangen genommen, jedoch nach 3 Tagen in ihre Heimatorte entlassen. Generalfeldmarschall von Rundstedt übermittelt Anerkennung OKW.

To preserve the honour of the flag, the French Admiral de Laborde sank almost the whole fleet, which France still had at her disposal. 73 ships sank, seven admirals and 27 000 marines were taken captive, but released in their home towns after three days. Field-Marshal von Rundstedt conveys the approbation of the OKW.

Die Ehre der Flotte
wahren die Franzosen.

The French maintain
the honour of the Fleet.

Die enge Hafeneinfahrt
von Toulon.

The narrow harbour mouth
of Toulon.

Die Kessel dieses Kreuzers
sind gesprengt.
Das Schiff
liegt auf Grund.

The boilers of this cruiser
are blown up.
The ship is grounded.

Von Frankreich anrollend, erreicht die Division im Eisenbahntransport Kiew.

Rolling from France, the division reached Kiev by rail transport. Off-loading of the Regimental Staff „Deutschland".

Sturmgeschütze auf dem Marsch.

SP assault-guns on the march.

Das neue Panzerregiment ist auch dabei. Die „Panther"-Abteilung ist noch in der Aufstellung in Frankreich geblieben.

The new Panzer Regiment is there too. The „Panther" Battalion is still forming up and stayed behind in France.

SS-Panzer-grenadier-Regiment „Deutschland" auf dem Marsch

Panzer Grenadier Regiment „Deutschland" on march

15. Krad-schützen-Kompanie im Schneesturm (15./SS. „D")

15 Motorcycle Infantry Company (15./SS „D") in a snow storm

Hanomag mit Allradlenkung und Zwillings-MG zur Tief-fliegerabwehr

„Hanomags" with allwheel-steering device and double-barrel MG against deep flying planes

Panzer und Sturm-geschütze zwischen den Panzer-grenadieren der 2. SS-Panzer-divison „Das Reich"

Panzers and S.Paussault guns between Panzer-Grenadiers of 2 SS Panzer Division „Das Reich"

Ende Januar traf die Division im Raum Kiew/Charkow ein und mußte sofort zum Donez. Dort war eine Lücke von fast 500 km entstanden.
Die vorstürmenden Spitzen der roten Gardepanzerarmee mußten gestoppt werden.

At the end of January, the division arrived in the Kiev/Kharkov area and had to go immediately to the Donez. A gap of almost 500 kms had appeared there. The forward storming spear-heads of the Red Guard Panzer Army had to be stopped.

Div. Gefechtsstand bei Tschugujew.

Divisional command post at Tschugujew.

Ausladung Teile Regiment „Deutschland" und Aufklärungs-Abt. in Kiew.

Parts of the Regiment „Deutschland" and Reconnaissance Battalion are off-loaded in Kiew.

III./gepanzertes Bataillon „Der Führer" und II. Abteilung Panzerregiment 2 im Angriff bei Woltschansk.

III/Armoured Battalion „Der Führer" and II Battalion Panzer Regiment 2 attacking at Woltschansk.

Der Gefechtsstand des SS-Panzergrenadier-Regiments „Deutschland" in Olchowatka am 31.1.43 ostwärts Charkow.

The battle H.Q. of the SS Panzer Grenadier Regiment „Deutschland" in Olchowatka on 31.1.43 east of Kharkov.

Abwehrkämpfe zwischen Don und Donez ostwärts Charkow.

Defensive fighting between Don and Donez east of Kharkov.

Vierlingsflak 2 cm auf Selbstfahrlafette am 4.2.43 bei Belikolodes.

A four-barrel 2 cm Flak on a self-propelled carriage, near Belikolodes.

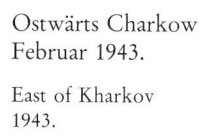

Ostwärts Charkow Februar 1943.

East of Kharkov 1943.

SS-Hauptsturmführer Dierks,
Adjutant Panzergrenadier-Regiment „Deutschland"
mit Ordonnanzoffizier Untersturmführer Braumandel
auf dem Gefechtsstand Anfang Februar 1943.

SS Hautsturmführer Dierks, adjutant of the Panzer
Grenadier Regiment „Deutschland" with the orderly officer
Untersturmführer Braumandel at the battle H.Q.
at the beginning of February 1943.

Die Truppe kämpft beweglich
gegen die vorstürmende Rote Armee.

The troops operate flexibly in their fight
against the forward thrusting Red Army.

Am 5.2.43 besetzt der Zug Doldi (11./„D") Wel-Burluk (erster Einsatz dieser Einheit).

On 5.2.43, Doldi's platoon (11./„D") captured Wel-Burluk (the first time in action of this unit).

Charkow wird geräumt,
am 15.2.43 um 13.00 Uhr wird Durchschlagen hinter dem Udy-Abschnitt befohlen,
da sonst Einschließung droht.

Kharkov is quitted on 15.2.43 at 13.00 hours,
a break-through is ordered behind the Udy sector as there is the threat of an encirclement.

Letzte Abwehrkämpfe ostwärts Charkow.

The last defensive fighting east of Kharkov.

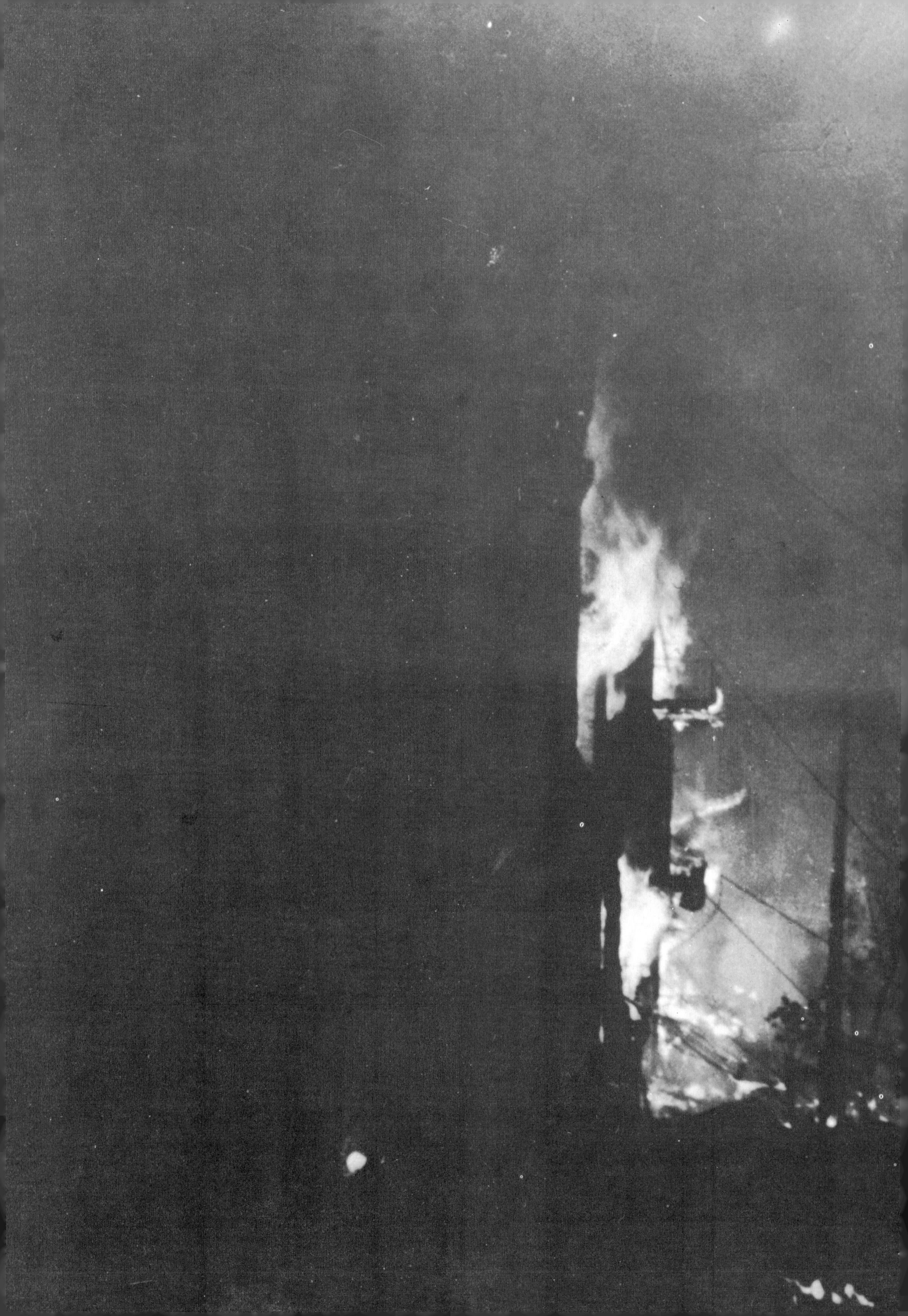

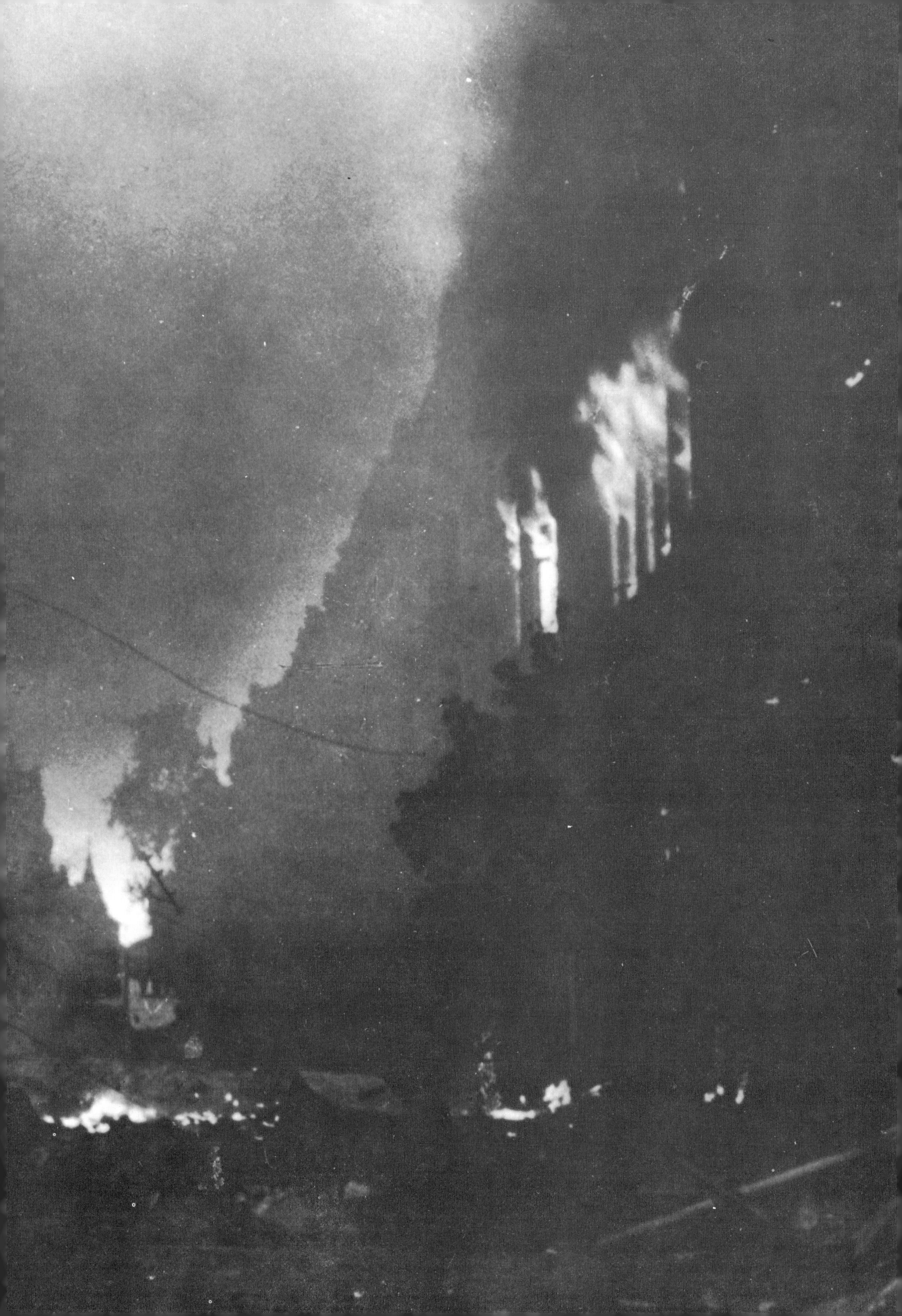

Nach ½ Stunde Schneesturm ist alles verweht.

Half-an-hour lasted the blizzard and everything was snow-covered.

Kradschützen vorausgeworfen.

Motor-cycle infantry sent forward.

„DF" am 13.2.43 im Vorgehen auf Borki.

„DF" on 13.2.43 advancing on Borki.

Ohne „Daunenbett" auf der Lafette der Pak 5 cm 38 nach vorn.

Without a „coverlet" on the gun-carriage of a Pak 5 cm 38, going forwards.

Abschrift.

Funkspruch Nr. 624   Absendende Stelle: Armee-Abt. **Lanz**
                                      Tag: 14.2.43
Dringend!   Zeit: 17,25 Uhr

Am

Generalkommando ᛋᛋ-Panzer-Korps

Panzer-Korps hält gemäß Führerbefehl bis zum letzten Mann
seine jetzige Stellung an der Ostfront von Charkow.

                                          gez. L a n z

F.d.R.d.A.

ᛋᛋ-Obersturmführer

According to „Führer's Order" Panzer-Corps holds its present position
on the eastern frontline of Kharkov to a man.

Straßenkampf in Charkow.
Am linken Bildrand Grenadier
mit magnetischer Hafthohlladung
(Panzer-Vernichter).

House to house fighting in Kharkov.
At the left side of the photograph
there is a grendier with a magnetic
limpet-bomb (tank-destroyer).

Letzte Befehle SS-Obersturmbannführer Harmel
zur Räumung Charkows
(Kommandeur Regiment „Deutschland").

The last orders of SS Obersturmbannführer Harmel on the evacuation of
Kharkov (commander of the Regiment „Deutschland").

Ordnung ist jetzt entscheidend. Harmel greift ein. Die Stunde seines Panzergrenadier-Regiments „Deutschland" kommt.
Orderliness is now the decisive factor. Harmel goes into action. The hour of his Panzer Grenadier Regiment „Deutschland" is coming.

Funker im Schützenpanzerwagen (SPW).

Radio operator in an armoured troop carrier (SPW).

Überall greift der Russe an.

The Russians attack from all sides.

Schweres Infanteriegeschütz der Division.

A heavy infantry gun of the division.

Gruppe Eps, 16./SS „D" (Infanteriepionierkompanie) räumt Minen. Bei verharschtem Schnee mehr Gefühl mit dem Seitengewehr als mit M-Suchgeräten, deren Batterien durch Kälte unbrauchbar waren. (19.2.43) Jeder Griff muß sitzen. (SS-Unterscharführer Eps gefallen Mai 1943)

The Group Eps, 16th/SS „D" (Infantry Pioneers Company) clears mines. Through the frozen snow crust, they can trace them better using side-arms than the mine detectors, the batteries of which were unusable because of the cold. But they can afford no mistakes (19.2.43). (SS-Unterscharführer Eps killed in action 5/1943)

Der vom Generalfeldmarschall von Manstein befohlene Angriff beginnt am 20.2.43

The attack ordered by Field-Marshal von Manstein begins on 20.2.43

und stößt am 22.2.43 nach Süden und Südwesten in den Rücken des Gegners.

and on 22.2.43 thrusts southwards and south westwards into the rear of the enemy.

Operationsfreiheit zurückgewonnen.
Feldmarschall v. Manstein gibt den Befehl,
die vorstürmenden sowjetischen Armeen im
Rücken anzugreifen.

Operational freedom regained. Field-Marshal
von Manstein gives the order to attack
the strongly advancing Soviet armies in the rear.

Alle bemühen sich
um den Schwerverwundeten.

Everyone makes an effort
for the badly wounded.

Nach Prikolotnotnoje
stoßen wir vor.

We push forward
to Prikolotnotnoje.

Besatzung eines abgeschossenen Kampfwagens (Rottenführer Barkmann) beritten zum Versammlungsraum.

The crew of a knocked out „Panther" ride on horseback to the assembly area.

Gert Schmager, Chef 9./„DF" bei Losowaja 25.2.43.

Auf der Rollbahn Nowo-Moskowsk-Pawlograd an brennendem T 34 vorbei mit Panzer IV der 3. Panzerkompanie.

On the route Nowo-Moskowsk-Pawlograd, past a burning T 34, with Panzer IVs of the 3rd Panzer Company.

... und noch ein T 34 vom Nachschub abgeschossen.

... and another T 34 shot up by the supply troops.

Der Stoß am 25.2.43 nach Losowaja schnitt die 6. russische Gardepanzer-Armee vom Nachschub ab.

On 25.2.43, the thrust to Losowaja cut off the 6th Russian Guard Panzer Army from its supply troops.

Sie ging der fast vollständigen Vernichtung entgegen.

It faced almost complete destruction.

Am 25.2.43 um 14 Uhr erreicht die Division Losowaja. Erbeutete Panzerspähwagen beim Regiment „DF".

On 25.2.43 at 14.00 hours the division reached Losowaja. Armoured scout cars captured by the Regiment „DF".

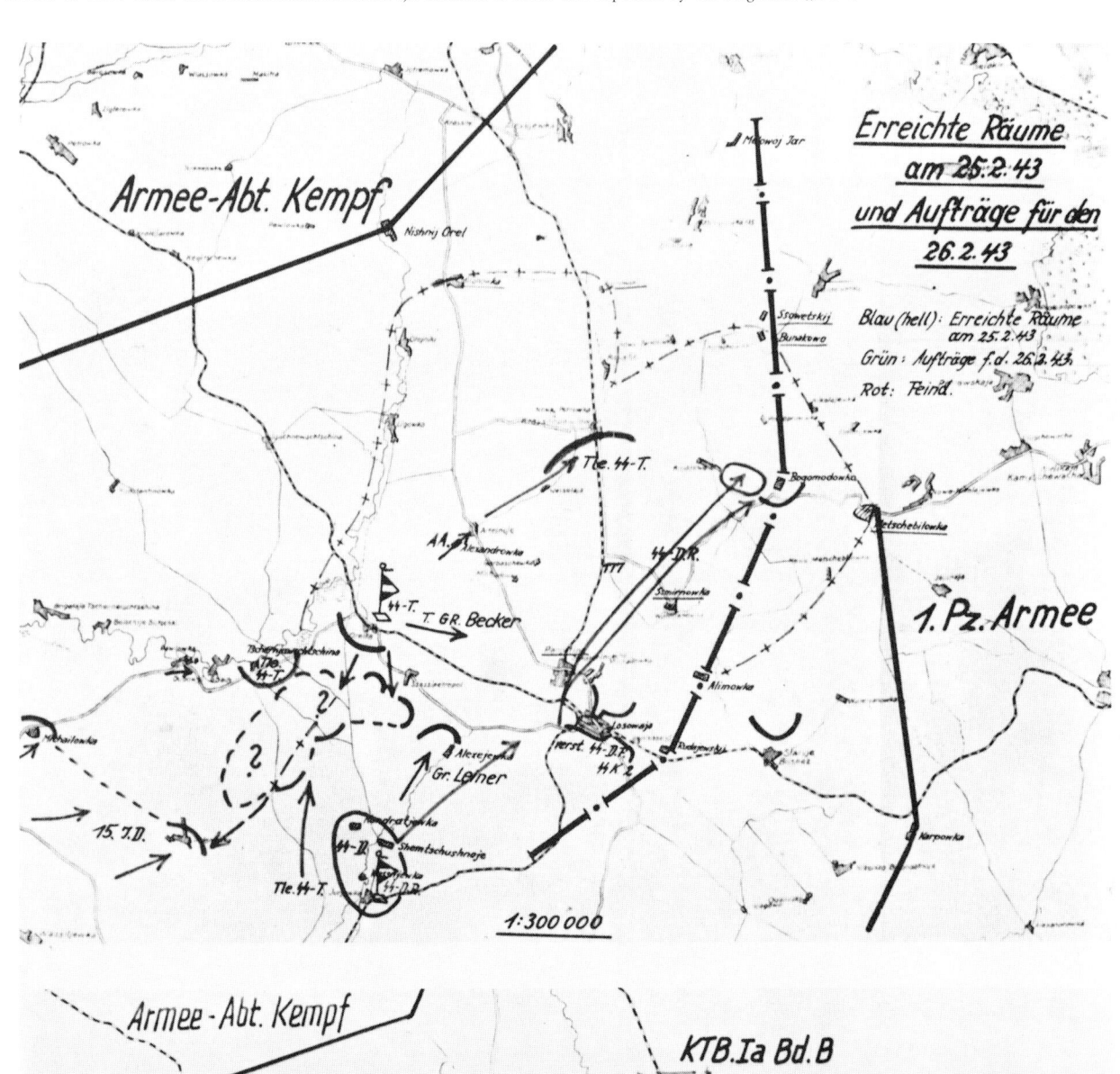

Vor ihrem Schützenpanzerwagen links Willi Scheer und rechts „Ferry" Fendt.

In front of their armoured troop carrier, Willi Scheer on the left and „Ferry" Fendt on the right.

Im Eis eingebrochener russischer Panzer T 34 bei Ochotschaya 4.3.43.

A smashed open Russian T 34 in the ice near Ochotschaya on 4.3.43.

Die ersten Sturmgeschütze erreichen am 12.3.43 den Standrand von Charkow und das III. Bataillon „DF" zieht in die Einbruchstelle am Panzergraben vor.

On 12.3.43, the first self-propelled guns reach the outskirts of Kharkov and the III Battalion „DF" follows into the break in point at the anti-tank ditch.

Kommandeur Rgt. „D", Heinz Harmel,
am 12.3.43 vor Charkow mit Vinzenz Kaiser, Kdr. III./(gep.) „DF".

Heinz Harmel, commander of the Regiment „D" on 12.3.43 in front of Kharkov with Vinzenz Kaiser, commander of III/(armoured) „DF".

Im erneuten Anmarsch auf Charkow.

Renewed advance on Kharkov.

Spitze Panzerregiment 2 wieder in den Vororten Charkows.

The spear-head Panzer Regiment 2 once again in the outskirts of Kharkov.

Aufklärungspanzer 14.3.43.

Scout panzer 14.3.43.

Im brusttiefen Schnee und großen Verwehungen trotzdem vorwärts.
In spite of knee-deep snow and huge snow-drifts onward.

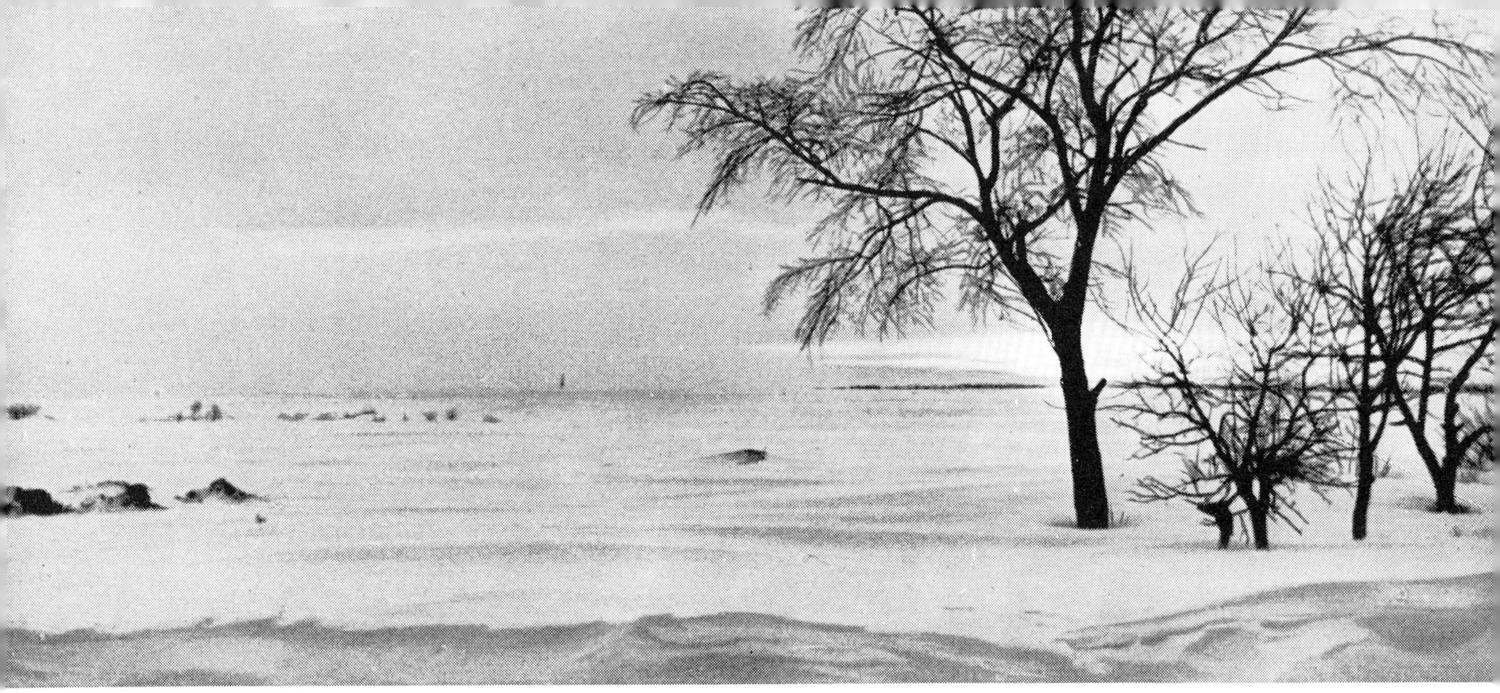
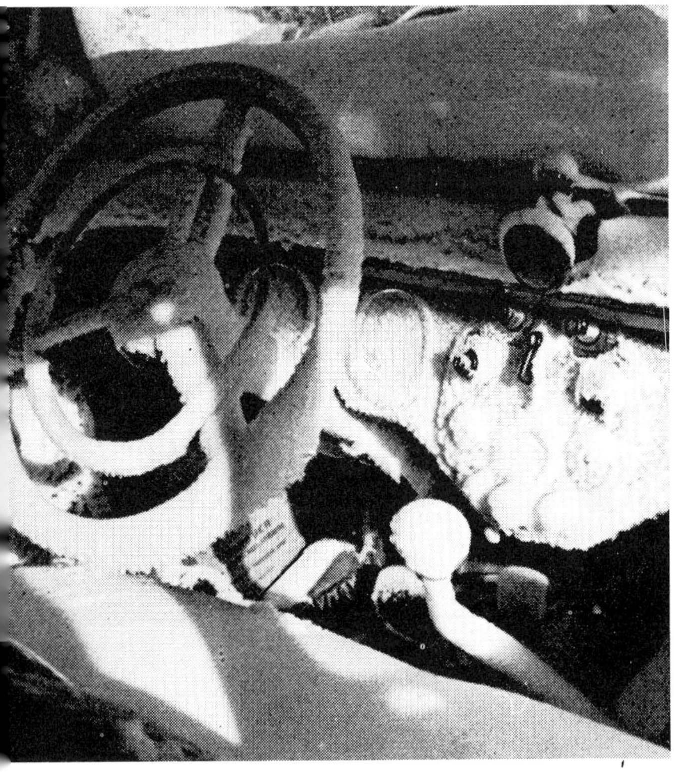
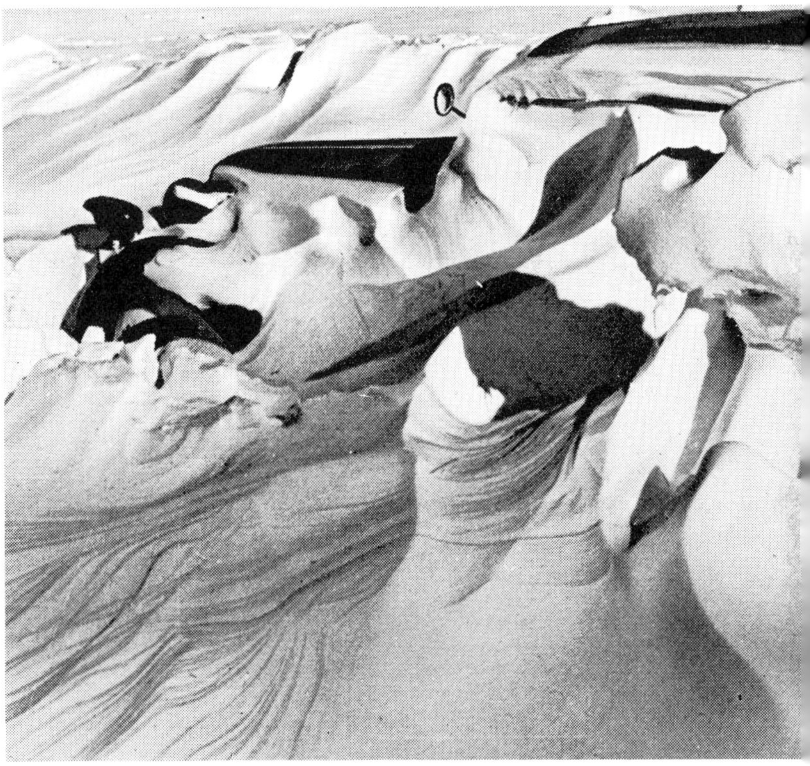
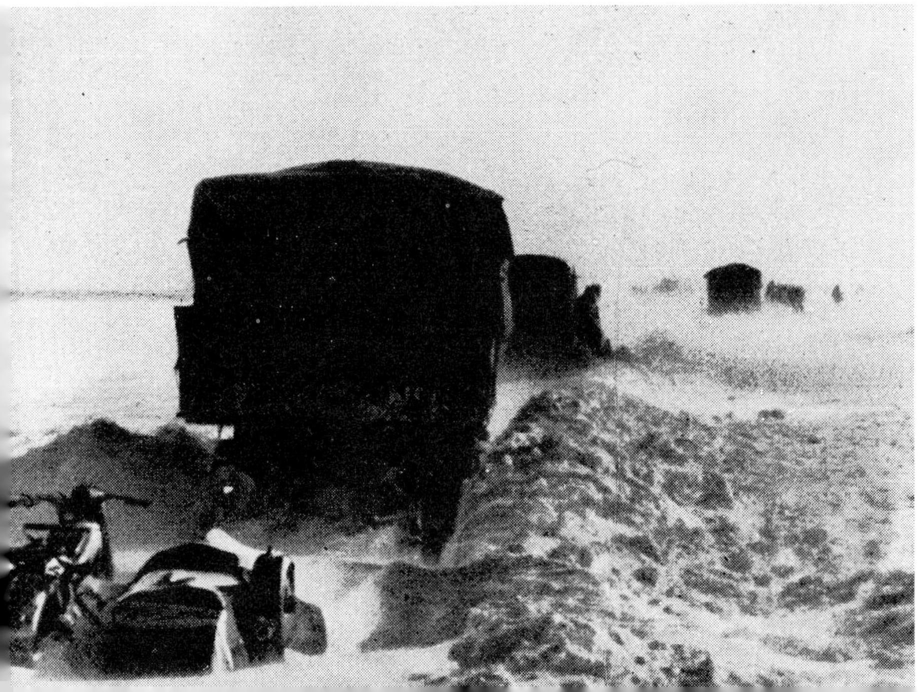
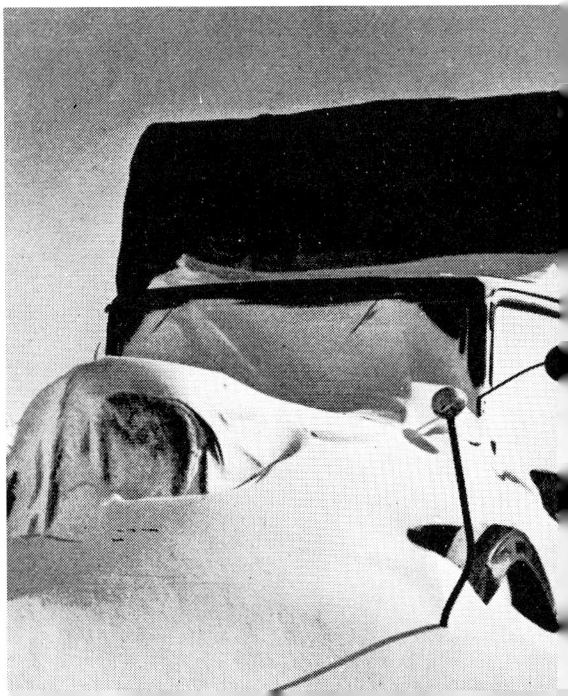

Das SS-Panzerkorps hat Charkow genommen:

The SS-Panzer-Corps conquered Kharkov:

1. die 1. SS-Panzerdivision „Leibstandarte" von Norden,

   the 1st SS Panzer Division „Leibstandarte" from north,

2. die 2. SS-Panzerdivision „Das Reich" von Westen,

   the 2nd SS Panzer Division „Das Reich" from west,

3. die 3. SS-Panzerdivision „Totenkopf" nach Osten überholend

   the 3rd SS Panzer Division „Totenkopf" outflanked eastward

SS-Brigadeführer und Generalmajor der Waffen-SS Vahl, für kurze Zeit Kommandeur Division „Das Reich". Er kam vom Heer zu uns.

SS Brigadeführer und Major-General Vahl (killed in action), for a short time commander of the Division „Das Reich". He came from the Army.

Unser Nachschub
bei Woroschilowgrad
ist am 15.3.43
auf erbeutete Schlitten
angewiesen.

At Woroschilowgrad on 15.3.43,
our supplies relied on captured sledges.

Die letzten Gefangenen
der 16. Komp. „DF"
bei Woroschilowgrad.

The latest prisoners
of the 16th Company „DF"
at Woroschilowgrad.

Der sowjetische
Nachtschlachtflieger
notgelandet bei Ssolomino
23.3.43.

The Soviet night fighter made an
emergency landing at Ssolomino on
23.3.43.

Nach der Wiedereinnahme Charkows ist die Bevölkerung freundlich.

After the recapture of Kharkov, the inhabitants are friendly.

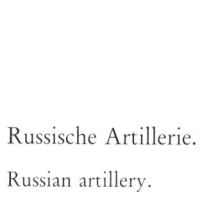

Russische Artillerie.

Russian artillery.

Zitadelle von Bjelgorod, gefallen am 18.3.43. Bjelgorod citadel fell on 18.4.43.

16./SS „D" mit Teilen beim Gefechtsstand des III./Rgt. „Deutschland".

16th/SS „D" with other troops at the command post of III/Regiment „Deutschland".

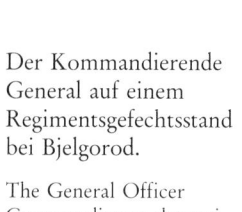

Der Kommandierende General auf einem Regimentsgefechtsstand bei Bjelgorod.

The General Officer Commanding at the regimental battle H.Q. at Bjelgorod.

Rast der Grenadiere bei Bjelgorod März 1943.

The grenadiers rest near Bjelgorod in March 1943.

Oberscharführer Neumann, Bildberichter bei der Division „Das Reich".

Oberscharführer Neumann, photo-correspondent with the Division „Das Reich".

Ukrainische Mädchen in Trachten,
Sommer 1943.

Ukrainian girls in their local costume,
summer 1943.

Truppenarzt Dr. Schmidt,
genannt „Kaninchen",
bei kleiner Hilfeleistung.

Medical Officer Dr. Schmidt,
nick named „Bunny Rabbit",
attends to a minor injury.

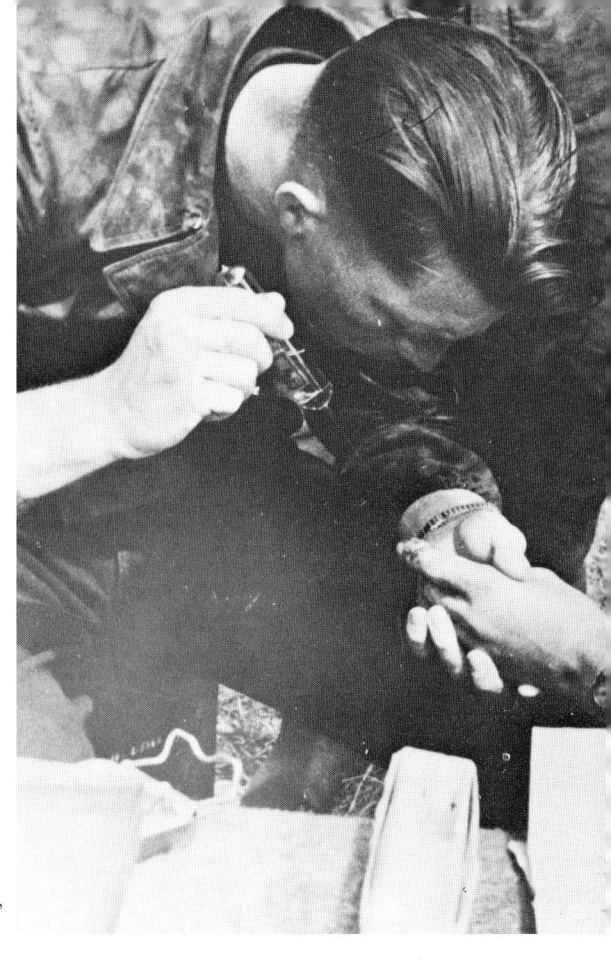

Fröhlich mit Gesang
ging es im Mai 1943 zu
bei der Aufstellung
der I. Abteilung
des 2. SS-Panzerregiments
„Das Reich"
in Mailly le Camp
bei Troyes (Panther).

Cheerful and singing
they went about their business
during the formation in May
1943 of the 1st Battalion of
the 2nd SS Panzer Regiment
„Das Reich" (Panther) in
Mailly le Camp near Troyes.

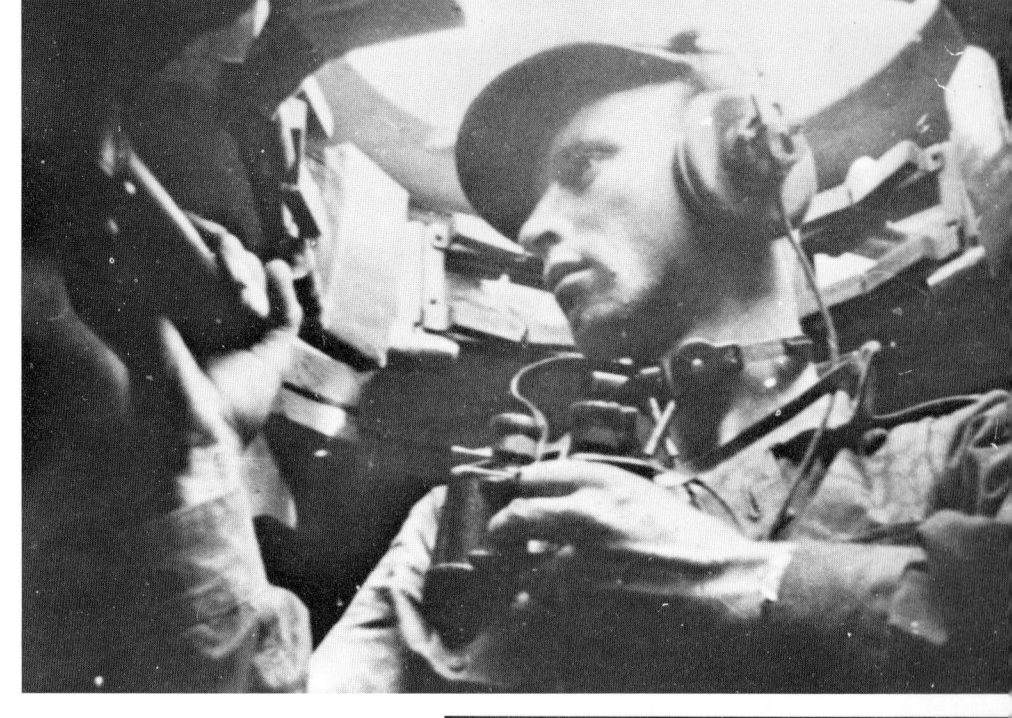

Panzerkommandant.

Panzer commander.

Panzerspäher
der Aufklärungs-Abteilung.

Armoured scout car-crew
of the Reconnaissance Battalion.

Panzergrenadiere beim Gurten
der Munition
für ihre Maschinengewehre.

Panzer grenadiers belting ammunition for machine-guns.

Der Kommandierende General des II. SS-Panzerkorps, SS-Obergruppenführer und General der Waffen-SS Paul Hausser, vor der Schlacht um den Frontbogen von Kursk mit Führern der Truppe.

The corps commander of the II SS Panzer Corps, SS Obergruppenführer and General of the Waffen SS Paul Hausser with troop commanders before the battle of the Kursk Salient.

5 cm Panzerabwehrgeschütz auf Selbstfahrlafette.

5 cm anti-tank gun on a self-propelled carriage.

225

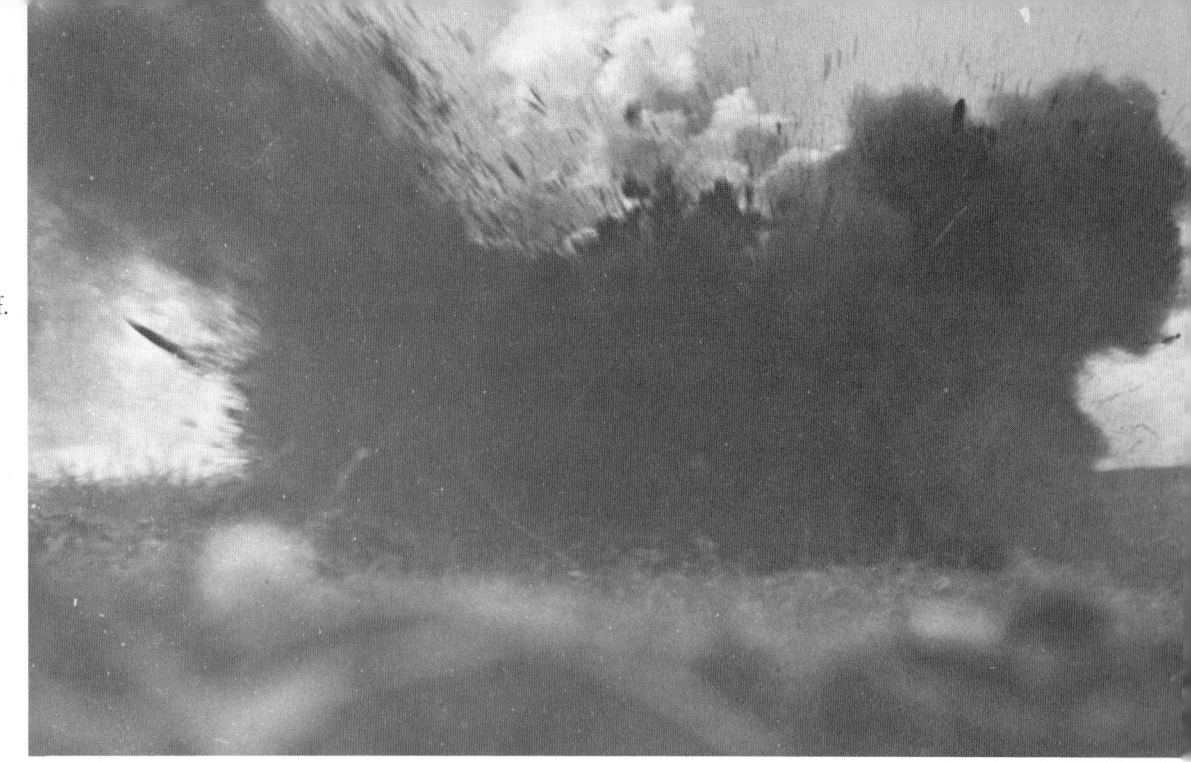

Am 5.7.43
beginnt der Angriff.

The attack begins
on 5.7.43.

Flammenwerfer
im Grabenkampf
um Beresoff.

Flame throwers
in trench fighting
around Beresoff.

Panzergrenadiere
und Pioniere
trugen die Hauptlast.

Panzer grenadiers
and pioneers
carried the principal burden.

Russische Panzer im Angriff.

Russian tanks attacking.

Deutsche Panzer IV nördlich Charkow.

German Panzer IV north of Kharkov.

Panzerkommandant Panzer VI „Tiger"
Kanone 8,8 cm.
Die 14 Ringe zeigen die Zahl der Abschüsse
gegnerischer Panzer an.

Panzer commander, Panzer VI „Tiger"
8,8 cm gun.
The 14 rings show the number of enemy
tanks knocked out.

Der Fahrer des 68 Tonnen wiegenden
Kampfwagens mit 700 PS-Motor.

The driver of the fighting vehicle weighing
68 tons with a 700 h.p. engine.

Der Richtschütze.

The gunner of the „Tiger".

Der Funker.

The radio operator.

Der Ladeschütze mit der 8,8 cm Kartuschengranate

The loader with the 8,8 cm shell

Im Panzergraben der Hauptverbandsplatz 5. Juli 1943 beim Unternehmen Zitadelle.

In the anti-tank ditch the main dressing station on 5th July 1943 during Operation Citadel.

Der Panzergraben von Beresoff ist am 1. Tag des Angriffs überwunden (5.7.43). Nachstoßen! Heinz Macher mit Pionieren.

The anti-tank ditch of Beresoff is overcome on the 1st day of the attack (5.7.43). Push on! Heinz Macher with pioneers.

Die Grenadiere im Grabenkampf um Beresoff.

The grenadiers in trench fighting around Beresoff.

Panzergrenadiere im Kampf um eine Ortschaft im Kursker Bogen.

Panzer grenadiers battle for a village in the Kursk salient.

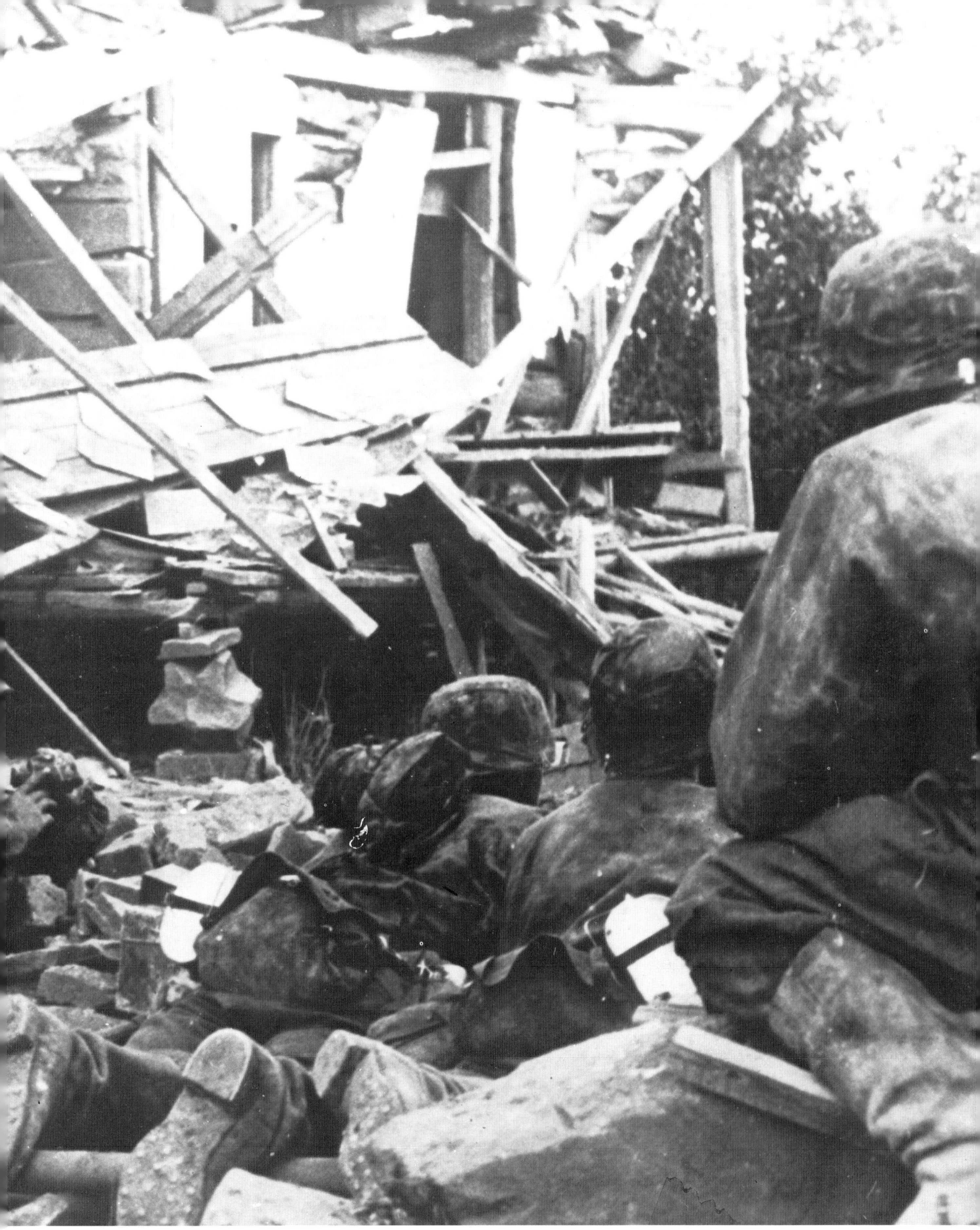

Eigene Panzer stehen am Hinterhang zum Angriff bereit.

Own tanks on the reverse slope, ready to attack.

Bekämfung russischer Schlachtflieger mit 2 cm Kanone.

Fighting Russian fighter 'planes with the 2 cm gun.

Panzer mit aufgesessenen Panzergrenadieren 8.7.43.

Panzer with panzer grenadiers seated on it on 8.7.43.

Die Rote Armee war gut vorbereitet.
Sie war über alles informiert.
Ihr fehlte nur das Datum und die Uhrzeit.
Es gab kein Überraschungsmoment.

The Red Army was well prepared.
It was informed about everything.
It lacked only the date and time.
Surprise was out of the question.

Das II. SS-Panzerkorps mit
„Das Reich" kämpfte
im Kursker Bogen
in der größten Panzerschlacht
der Geschichte.

The II. SS Panzer Corps with „Das Reich"
fought in the greatest tank battle
of history, in the Kursk salient.

SS-Untersturmführer Burfeind
mit seinen Männern
bei Michailowka am 10.7.43.

SS Untersturmführer Burfeind
with his men at Michailowka on 10.7.43.

Die Wasserstelle.

Water point.

Abgeschossener T 34.

A knocked out T 34.

15 cm Werferbatterien
im Feuerkampf.

15 cm mortar battery
firing in battle.

Vor dem Einsatz.
Bei jedem Halt
sofort „in die Erde".

Before going into action.
They „go to earth"
at every halt.

Gefechtsstand bei Ternowoje
mit „Tiger"
bei Munitionsübernahme.

Command post at Ternowoje.
A „Tiger" collects ammunition.

Essenholer mit Thermoskübel.

Food carrier with thermos container.

Schweres Infanteriegeschütz
auf Selbstfahrlafette („Grille")

Heavy infantry gun on a self-propelled
carriage („Grille")

Sturmgeschütz
unterstützt
die Grenadiere.

Grenadiers
with support
of an assault gun.

Das Kampffeld mit unseren „Tiger"-Panzern und den weit auseinandergezogenen Grenadieren.
The battlefield with our „Tiger" panzers and the widely diverged grenadiers.

Sturmgeschütz mit
Kanone 7,5 cm lang.

Assault gun with
7,5 cm gun, local barrel.

2 cm-Flak
im Erdziel-Beschuß.

2 cm Flak
shooting at ground target.

v.l.n.r.: SS-Standartenführer Harmel,
SS-Obersturmführer Dorbath
(Waffen- u. Mun.-Offz.)

from l. to r.: SS-Standartenführer Harmel,
SS-Obersturmführer Dorbath
(Waffen- u. Mun.-Offz.)

SS-Sturmbannführer Günther-Eberhardt
Wisliceny, Kommandeur III./„D"

SS Sturmbannführer Günther-Eberhardt
Wisliceny, Commander III/„D"

und SS-Hauptsturmführer Sperling,
Verwaltungsführer am Mius,
vor dem Gefecht.

and SS-Hauptsturmführer Sperling
administration officer before the battle
at the river Mius.

Bei Stepanowka am Mius —
letzter Erfolg im Osten.

At Stepanowka on the Mius —
the last success in the East.

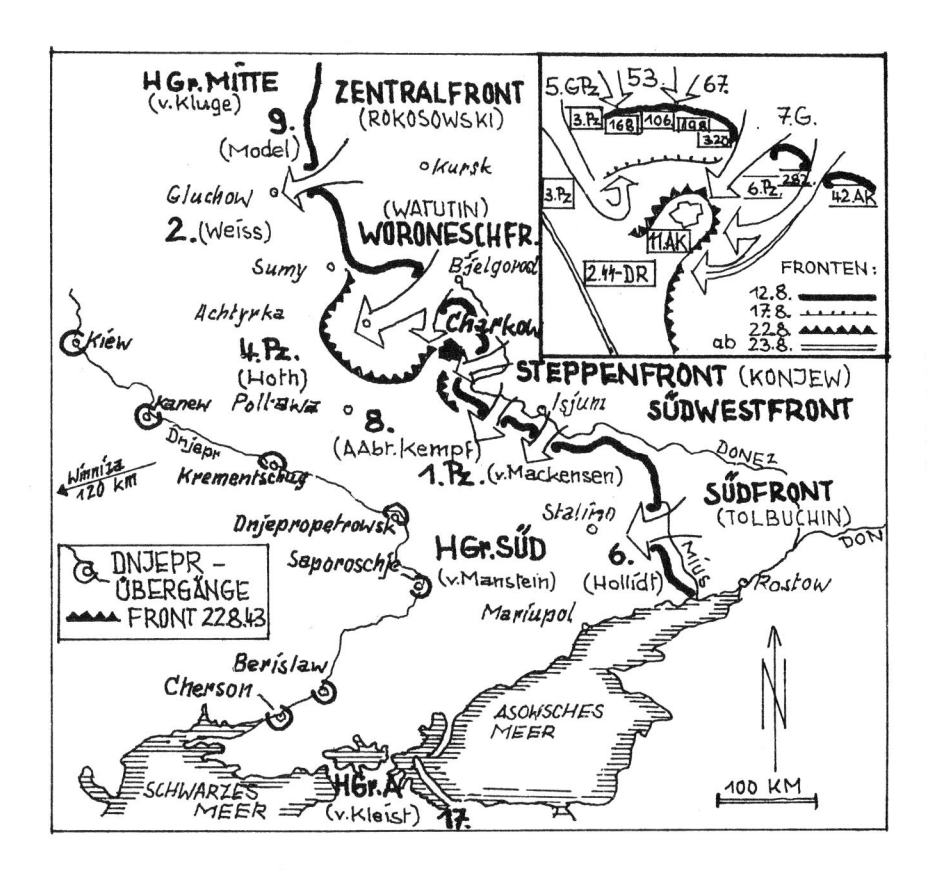

Zwischen Mius und Dnjepr.

Between the Mius and Dnieper.

Verdeckte Abwehrstellung am Mius.   A concealed defensive position on the Mius.

Der Kommandeur, SS-Sturmbannführer Wisliceny, III./„D", und SS-Hauptsturmführer Schreiber, Chef der 10. Kompanie, im gemeinsamen Schützenloch.

The commander SS Sturmbannführer Wisliceny III/„D", and SS Hauptsturmführer Schreiber, head of the 10th Company, together in a foxhole.

Die SS-Obersturmführer Rothermund und Pilz (gefallen als Chef der 4. Panzerkompanie),
SS-Hauptscharführer Reichenbecher,
SS-Untersturmführer Hargesheimer,
SS-Unterscharführer Haslinger
August 1943.

SS Obersturmführers Rothermund and Pilz (killed in action as commander of 4th Company),
SS Hauptscharführer Reichenbecher,
SS Untersturmführer Hargesheimer,
SS Unterscharführer Haslinger
August 1943.

Tarnung in der Bereitstellung.

Camouflage during final assembly.

T 34 nach Volltreffer vernichtet (4. Kompanie).

T 34 destroyed by direct hit (4th Company).

SS-Unterscharführer Johann Thaler, 6. Kompanie des Panzerjägerregiments, erhält als 1. Panzerfahrer am 17.8.43 das Ritterkreuz.

On 17.8.43 SS Unterscharführer Johann Thaler, 6th Company of the Anti-Tank Regiment was the first panzer driver to receive the Knight's Cross.

Russischer Panzerjäger auf Selbstfahrlafette, Kaliber 7,62 cm, am 26.8.43 bei Korotisch erbeutet.

Russian anti-tank gun on self-propelled carriage, calibre 7,62 cm, was captured on 26.8.43 at Korotisch.

Russisches 17,2 cm Sturmgeschütz bei Nikotowka außer Gefecht gesetzt.

Russian 17,2 cm assault gun put out of action at Nikotowka.

Bereitstellung unserer
„Tiger"-Panzer, der „Panther"
und Panzer IV.

Our „Tiger" panzers, the „Panthers"
and the Panzers IV assemble.

Lage bei Korotisch wird besprochen.

The situation at Korotisch is discussed.

Am 26.8.43 bei Korotisch ein leichtes Infanteriegeschütz im Feuerkampf.

A light infantry gun firing in battle at Korotisch on 26.8.43.

Grenadiere gehen in die Bereitstellung.

Grenadiers prepare to go into action.

Panzerspähwagen überqueren auf einem Fährprahm den Dnjepr.

Armoured scout cars cross the Dnieper on a ferry barge.

Nach der Panzerschlacht am 12. und 13.9.43 bleiben 78 russische Panzer vernichtet auf dem Gefechtsfeld liegen.

After the tank battle on 12 and 13.9.43, 78 Russian tanks lie destroyed on the battlefield.

Von links nach rechts:
SS-Oberscharführer Hund — Kradstaffelführer
SS-Hauptsturmführer Drexler — Chef 4. Kompanie
SS-Obersturmführer Prix — Abteilungs-Adjutant
SS-Sturmbannführer Weidinger — Kommandeur der Aufklärungs-
    Abteilung „Das Reich".

From left to right:
SS Oberscharführer Hund — Motorcycle Troop Commander
SS Hauptsturmführer Drexler — Commander 4th Company
SS Obersturmführer Prix — Adjutant Battalion
SS Sturmbannführer Weidinger — Commander of the Reconnaissance
    Battalion „Das Reich".

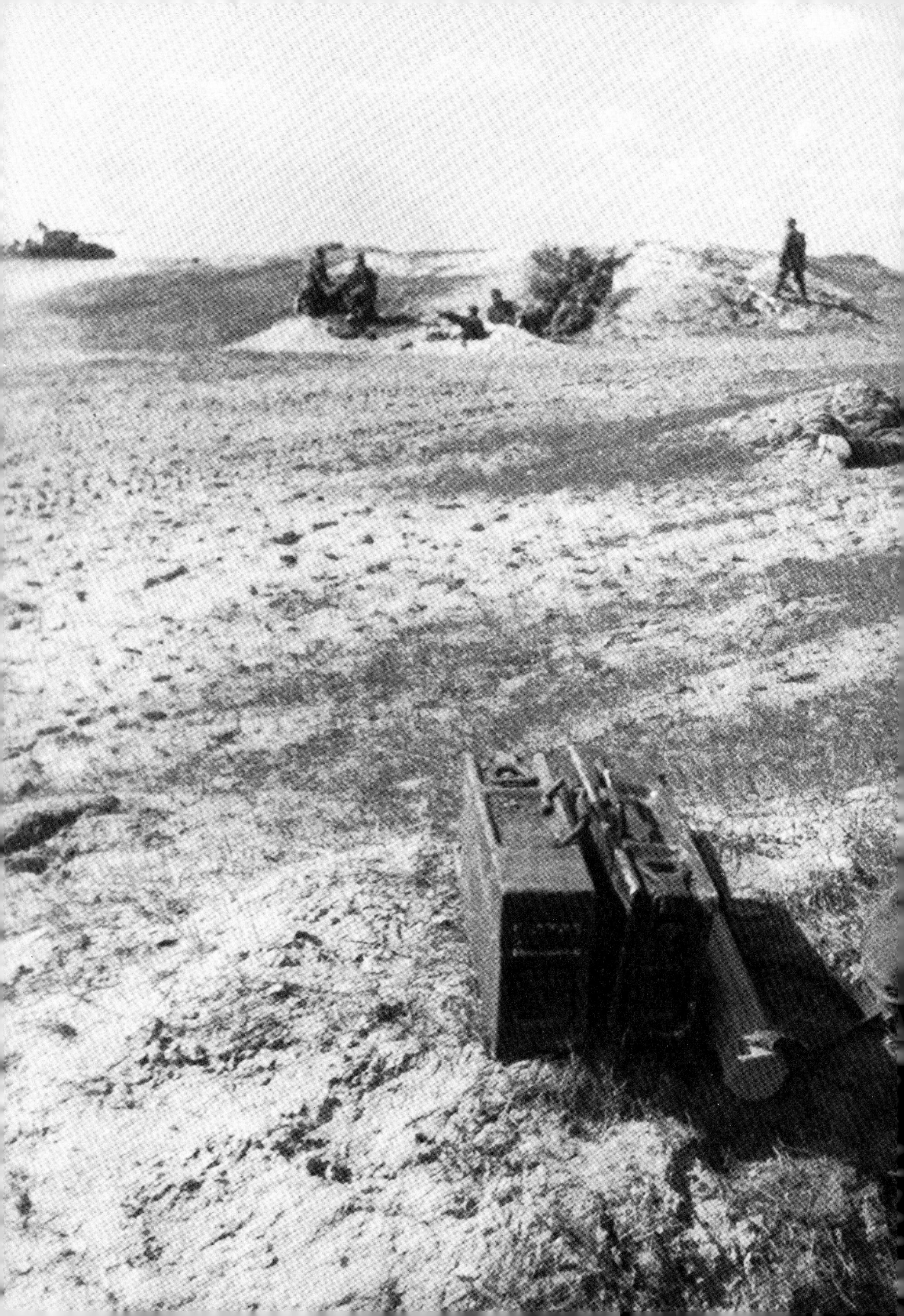

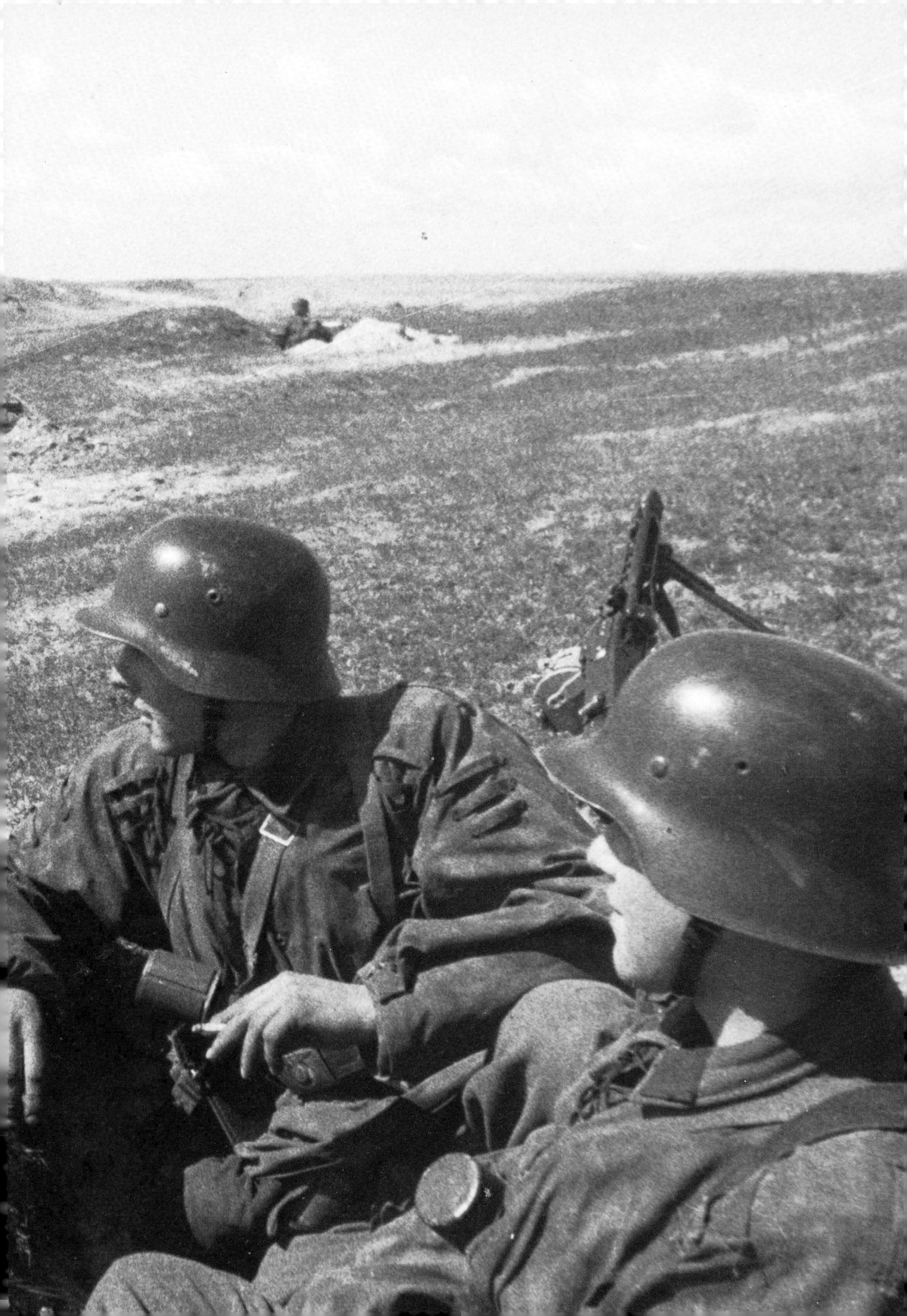

Das Ende der Brücke von Krementschug September 1943.

The end of Krementschug bridge September 1943.

1. von links Dr. Schlink, Div.-Arzt, 2 von links Walter Krüger, Kommandeur Division „Das Reich" (Eichenlaub z. Ritterkreuz 31.8.43), 3. von links Karl Kreutz, Kommandeur Artillerieregiment (DR), 4. von links Sorg, Kommandeur Nachr.Abt., 5 von links Silvester Stadler, Kommandeur Panzergrenadier-Rgt. „DF" (Eichenlaub 15.9.43).

1rst left Dr. Schlink, divisional doctor, 2nd from left Walter Krüger, divisional-commander Division „Das Reich" (Knight's Cross with Oakleaves 31.8.43), 3rd from left Karl Kreutz, commanding-officer Artillery-Regiment (DR), 4th from left Sorg, commanding officer of the Signals-Battalion, 5th from left Silvester Stadler, commanding-officer Panzer-Grenadier-Regiment „DF" (Knight's Cross with Oakleaves 15.9.43).

Div. "Das Reich" bei 8. Armee geht bei Krementschug über den Dnjepr.

Am schweren Maschinengewehr.

With a heavy machine-gun.

Sturmgeschütz in der Panzerschlacht am Mius.

Assault gun in the tank battle on the Mius.

251

Frugales Mittagessen in der Abwehrstellung der Aufklärungs-Abteilung 2. Im Vordergrund: Adjutant Aufklärungs-Abt. 2, Obersturmführer Prix (gefallen).

A frugal lunch in the defensive position of Reconnaissance Battalion 2. In the foreground: the Adjutant of Reconnaissance Battalion 2, Obersturmführer Prix (killed in action).

Ausgebrannter ‚Panther' und das Feldgrab der Besatzung Unterscharführer Kneusgen 4./Pz.Rgt. bei Krementschug.

A burnt out 'Panther' and the battlefield grave of the crew with Unterscharführer Kneusgen 4./Pz.Rgt. at Krementschug.

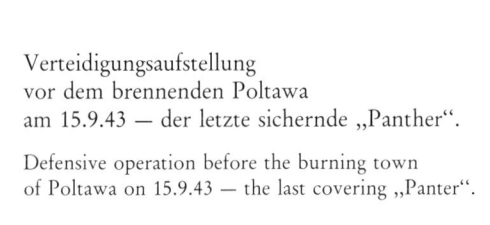

Verteidigungsaufstellung vor dem brennenden Poltawa am 15.9.43 — der letzte sichernde „Panther".

Defensive operation before the burning town of Poltawa on 15.9.43 — the last covering „Panter".

Hinterhangstellung getarnter Kampfwagen „Panther" des 2. SS-Panzerregiments „Das Reich".

A camouflaged „Panther" of 2nd SS Panzer Regiment „Das Reich" in a reverse slope position.

Lage am 1.12.1943 — 19.00 Uhr

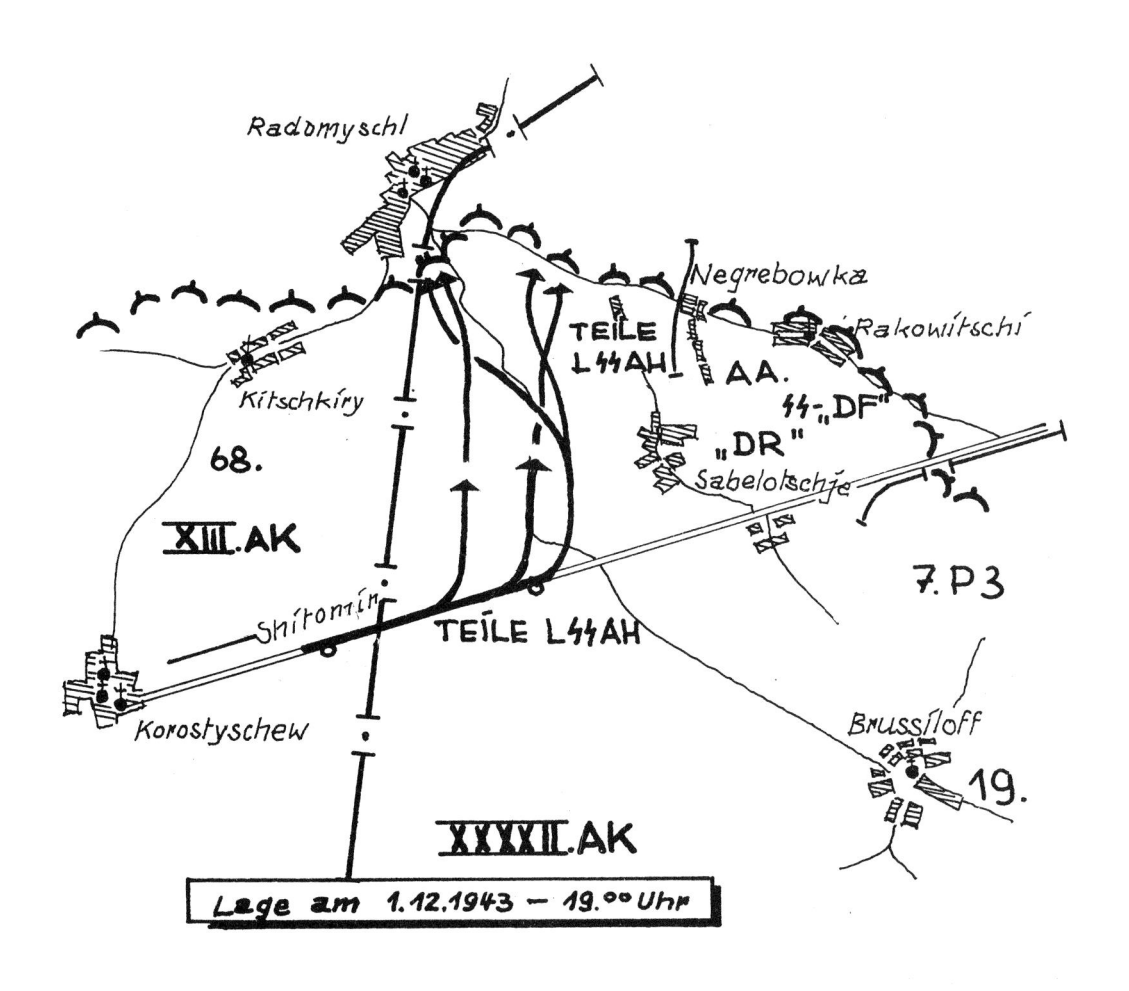

Verlegungsmarsch mit der Bahn.
Tieffliegerabwehr.

Proceeding to another position by train.
Protection against low-flying fighters.

Unsere „Tiger"
ostwärts Shitomir
auf dem Marsch.

Our „Tigers"
east of Shitomir
on the move.

Der Generalinspekteur der Panzertruppen bei der 2. SS-Panzerdivision
kurz vor der Landung der Alliierten in der Normandie
bei der Kritik anläßlich der Übung.
Generaloberst Guderian kannte uns sehr gut.
Dahinter Kommandeur des Panzerregiments 2 „Das Reich",
Obersturmbannführer Tychsen (gefallen).

The General Inspector of the Panzer Troops with the 2nd SS Panzer Division
during the critical analysis of an exercise shortly
before the Allied landing in Normandy.
Colonel-General Guderian knew us very well.
Behind, commander of Panzer Regiment 2 „Das Reich",
Obersturmbannführer Tychsen (killed in action).

5. Kompanie, 3. Zug, 5. Wagen = ergab die Nr. 535.

5th Company, 3rd Platoon, 5th Vehicle
resulted in the number 535.

Im Mai 1944 besuchte Generaloberst Guderian in Montauban (Südfrankreich) die Division, deren Kommandeur, SS-Brigadeführer und Generalmajor der Waffen-SS Lammerding, ihm vorträgt.

In Mai 1944, Colonel-General Guderian visited the division in Montauban (Southern France), which is presented to him by its commander SS Brigadeführer und Major-General Lammerding.

Bei einer Besichtigung in der Normandie:
Sturmbannführer Kämpfe erklärt dem Kommandierenden General (Heer) die eigene Lage.

During an inspection in Normandy:
Sturmbannführer Kämpfe explains the own situation to the commanding general (German Army).

255

Panzerkommandanten.

Panzer commanders.

Schulgefechtsschießen der Panzer V „Panther" Mai 1944 Südfrankreich (Caussade).

Panzer V „Panther" on shooting exercises in Southern France (Caussade) May 1944.

Panzer-Regiment — Übung in Caussade.
Mit Ritterkreuz: Sturmbannführer Kesten, gefallen Abteilungs-Kommandeur Panzerregiment 2 „Das Reich".

Panzer Regiment — Training in Caussade.
With the Knight's Cross: Sturmbannführer Kesten (killed in action) Battalion Commander Panzer Regiment 2 „Das Reich".

Der Regiments-Kommandeur
SS-Obersturmbannführer Christian Tychsen,
wenig später in der Normandie-Schlacht gefallen,
verleiht Auszeichnungen für Tapferkeit.

The Regimental Commander
SS Obersturmbannführer Christian Tychsen,
killed a short time later in the Normandy battle,
confers decorations for bravery.

Der Regimentsstander zwischen den „Panthern".

The regimental standard between the „Panthers".

„General der Panzertruppen West"
Freiherr Geyr von Schweppenburg,
ihm unterstanden alle Panzerverbände im Westen.
Sein Stab fiel bei einem starken Bombenangriff voll aus.

„General of Panzer Troops West"
Freiherr Geyr von Schweppenburg,
he was charge of all panzer troops in the west.
His whole staff was wiped out in a heavy bomb attack.

Auch Generaloberst von Blaskowitz
nahm an einer Verbandsübung
vor Beginn der Invasion 1944 teil.

Colonel-General von Blaskowitz also participated
in a troop exercise before the start of the 1944 Invasion.

SS-Sturmmann Mahn, von Maquisards erschossen, wird am 2.6.44 beigesetzt. Kameraden seiner Kompanie (16./„D") tragen ihn zu Grabe.

SS Sturmmann Mahn, shot by the Maquisards, is buried. Comrades from his company (16th/„D") bear him to his grave.

SS-Obersturmführer Heinz Macher mit den Unterführern der 16. Kompanie „Deutschland" 2.6.44.

SS Obersturmführer Heinz Macher with N.C.O.s of the 16th Company „Deutschland", 2.6.44.

SS-Sturmbannführer Kämpfe
(RK 10.12.43), Kommandeur
des III. gepanzerten Bataillons Regiment
„DF", wurde mit anderen Soldaten
der Division am 9. Juni 1944
von Marquisards ermordet.
Bei der Suche nach ihm
kam die 3. Kompanie nach
Oradour sur Glane.
In der Regimentsgeschichte „DF"
„Kameraden bis zum Ende"
wird darüber berichtet.

SS Sturmbannführer Kämpfe
(Knight's Cross 10.12.43), Commander
of III Armoured Battalion, Regiment
„DF", was murdered with other soldiers
of the division on 9th June 1944
by the Maquisards.
During the search for him,
the 3rd Company
came to Oradour sur Glane.
There will be an account of this
in the history of the Regiment „DF"
„Kameraden bis zum Ende".

SS-Oberscharführer Ellwanger
10.7.44 nach Verpflegungsempfang.
Bei Vernichtung eines
Sherman-Panzers der Amerikaner
am 11.7.44 gefallen.

SS Oberscharführer Ellwanger
after receiving rations 10.7.44.
He was killed, destroying
a Sherman tank of the Americans
on 11.7.44.

Lauerstellung
zwischen den Knicks
in der Normandie.

Lying in wait
among the hedgerows
in Normandy.

SS-Rottenführer Allard in einer Gefechtspause.
Neben ihm ein typisches Faß für die Aufbewahrung des normannischen Apfelweines, dem Cidre.

SS Rottenführer Allard during a break in the battle. Next to him, a typical barrel for storing „Cidre", the Normandy apple wine.

Leichtes Flakgeschütz auf Selbstfahrlafette
bekämpfte vorwiegend die Schwärme
der Jagdbomber,

A light anti-aircraft gun on a self-propelled carriage
operated predominantly against the swarms
of fighter-bombers,

→

Angreifende deutsche
Panzer im Sperrfeuer.

Attacking German
tanks in a barrage.

denen am 23.7.44 unser Oberbefehlshaber
der Heeresgruppe West,
Generalfeldmarschall Erwin Rommel,
zum Opfer fiel und schwerverwundet ausschied.

to which our Commander-in-Chief of Army Group West,
Field-Marshal Erwin Rommel fell victim on 23.7.44
and withdrew heavily wounded from active service.

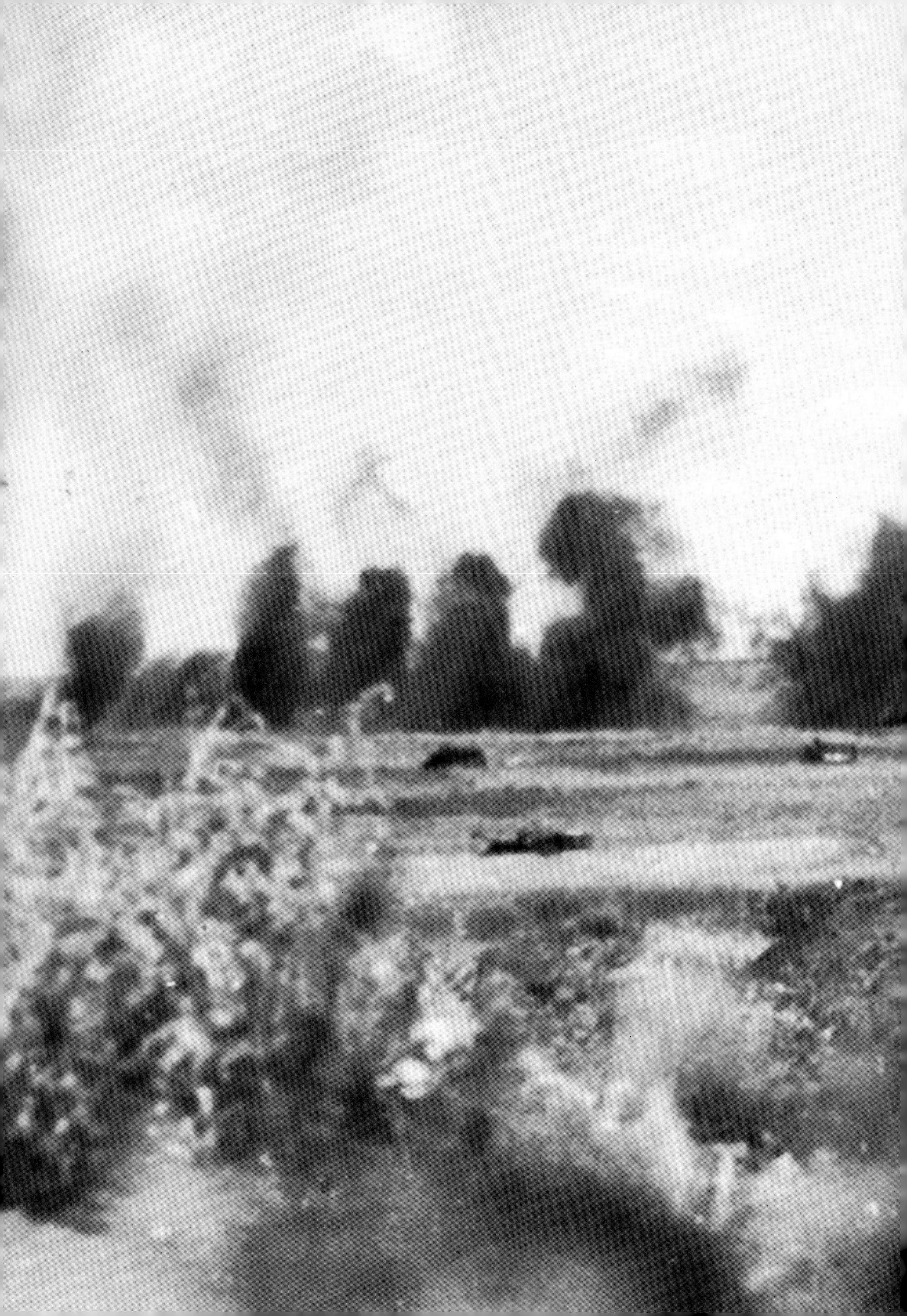

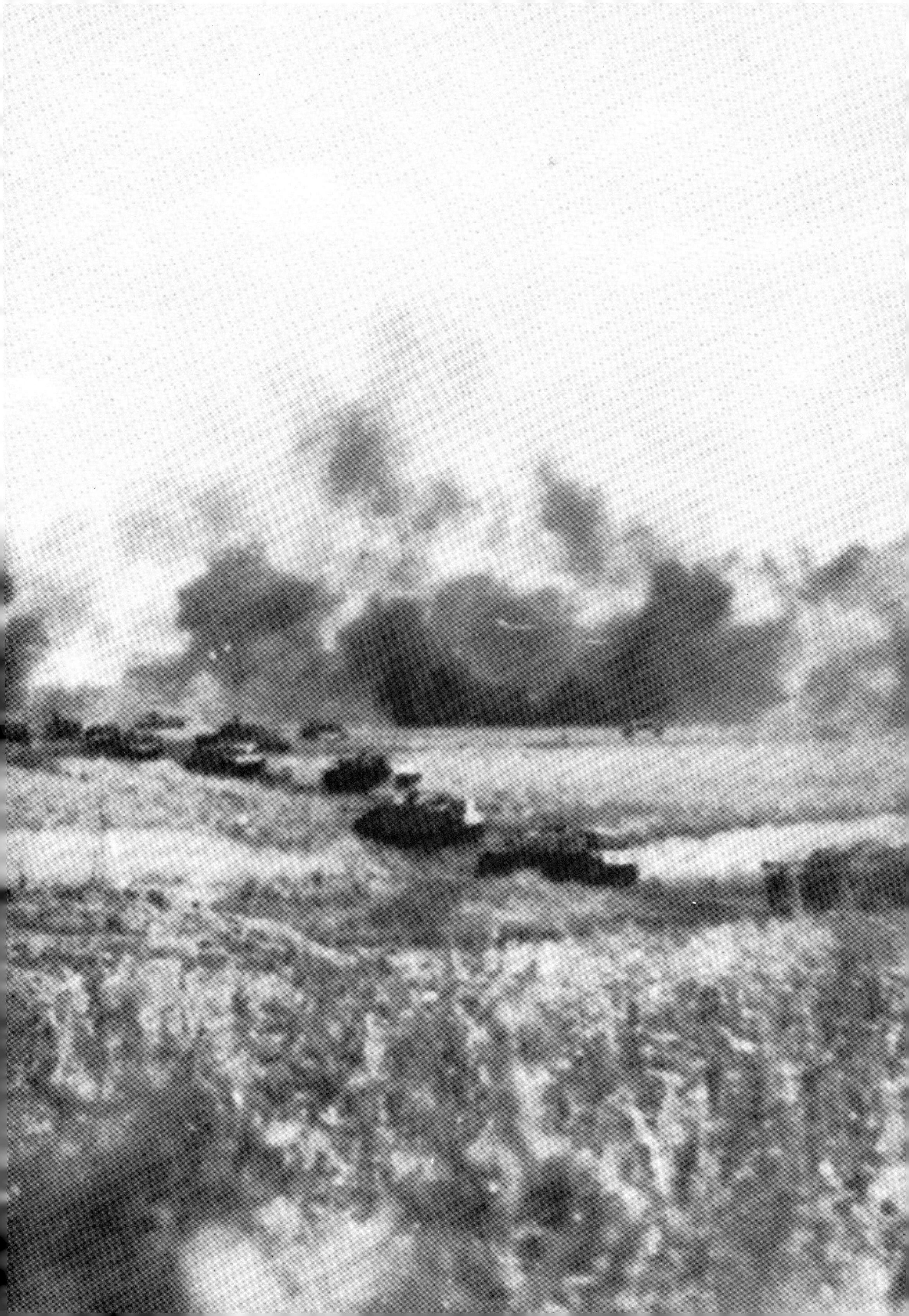

Der Divisionskommandeur
und seine Ordonnanzoffiziere
beobachten feindliche Flieger, die die totale
Luftherrschaft besaßen. Die eigene Luftwaffe schien
nicht mehr existent. Der Himmel war offen;
motorisierte Verbände verloren die operative
und taktische Beweglichkeit.

The divisional commander and his adjutants observe the
enemy aircrafts which possessed total air superiority.
Our own Luftwaffe did not seem to exist any more.
The sky was open; motorized troops lost their operational
and tactical manoeuvrability.

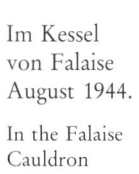

Im Kessel
von Falaise
August 1944.

In the Falaise
Cauldron
August 1944.

— „Panther" des SS-Panzerregiments 2
— „Panther" of SS Panzer Regiment 2

und Panzer IV eingegraben und abgeschossen.
and a dug-in and knocked out Panzer IV.

Vernichteter amerikanischer Schaufelpanzer.

Destroyed American tank with shoveling device.

Hinten im Kübelwagen Wisliceny mit Regimentsadjutant Hans Sailer, der wenige Minuten nach dieser Aufnahme bei einem Fliegerangriff fiel.

In the rear of the „Kübelwagen" (jeep) the Rgt.Adjutant Hans Sailer who was killed in action a few minutes later by an air raid.

Am 16.8.44 über die Seine bei Rouen. Pi.Batl. hatte die Brücke passierbar gemacht. Kommandeur G.E. Wisliceny überwacht das Übersetzen.

Crossing of the Seine near Rouen 16.8.44.
Pioneer Battalion repaired the bridge.
The Commander, G.E. Wisliceny, supervises the crossing.

SS-Hauptscharführer Adolf Peichl vom III./„DF" wurde wegen Tapferkeit SS-Untersturmführer (Ritterkreuz 16.10.1944). Er hat 6 Panzer als Einzelkämpfer vernichtet.

SS Hauptscharführer Adolf Peichl of III/„DF" was promoted to SS Untersturmführer for his courage (Knight's Cross 16.10.1944). He single-handedly destrstroyed six tanks.

Im September 1944 erhielten auf dem Gefechtsstand des Panzerartillerie-Regiments 2 „Das Reich" bei Prüm/Eifel dessen Kommandeur, SS-Standartenführer Karl Kreutz und SS-Oberscharführer Hans Schabschneider, Munitionsstaffelführer 5. Batterie des Regiments, vom SS-Standartenführer Otto Baum als Divisionsführer das Ritterkreuz.

In September 1944 at the command post of the Panzer Artillery Regiment 2 „Das Reich" in Prüm/Eifel, its commander SS Standartenführer Karl Kreutz and SS Oberscharführer Hans Schabschneider, ammunition staff commander 5th Battery of the Regiment, received the Knight's Cross from SS Standartenführer Otto Baum as divisional commander.

In den
Ruinen
von Argentan.

In the
ruins
of Argentan.

270

Angeschossener
„Panther",
dem ein
amerikanisches
Pak-Geschoß die
18 cm starke
Walzenblende
und die Optik
beschädigte.

The „Panther" is
hit, shot
by an American
anti-tank gun
which damaged
the armour
plating
and gunnery
optics.

Kommandeur des SS-Panzer-Grenadier-Regiments „Der Führer" — 4. SS-Panzergrenadier-Regiment — SS-Obersturmbannführer Otto Weidinger zeichnet am 9.11.44 anläßlich der Rekrutenvereidigung bewährte Soldaten aus.

The commander of the SS Panzer Grenadier Regiment „Der Führer" — 4th SS Panzer Grenadier Regiment — SS Obersturmbannführer Otto Weidinger decorates soldiers who have distinguished themselves, on the occasion of the swearing-in of recruits.

271

Männer einer Motorrad-Einheit bereiten sich auf eine Aufklärungspatrouille vor. Der Munitionsgürtel des MG40 Maschinengewehres wird überprüft.

Men from a Waffen-SS motor cycle unit prepare to go on a reconnaissance patrol. The MG40 machine gun has its ammunition belt checked.

Die deutsche Luftwaffe ist erstmals am Himmel. Amerikaner schauen hinauf.
The German Luftwaffe appears in the sky for the first time. Americans look up.

„Tiger" in der Eifel. Während der Ardennenoffensive brach die Versorgung zusammen.
A „Tiger" in the Eifel. The supply system collapsed during the Ardennes Offensive.

Durchfurcht von Panzerketten und Granaten ist die Erde. Es geht um die eingeschlossenen SS-Kavalleriedivisionen „Florian Geyer" und „Maria Theresia" und andere in Budapest. Ende Januar/Anfang Februar vor Budapest.

The earth is ploughed up by tracks and shells. It concerns the encircled SS Cavalry Divisions „Florian Geyer" and „Maria Theresia" and others in Budapest. End of Januara/beginning of February in front of Budapest.

Panzer IV in Feuerstellung,
Anfang Februar 1945.

Panzer IV in a firing position,
beginning of February, 1945.

Die Sowjets werden mit 12 cm Granatwerfern niedergehalten.

The Soviets are kept down with 12 cm mortars.

Der Versuch, die Besetzung Budapests
zu entsetzen, ist gescheitert.
Die Materialüberlegenheit des Feindes ist enorm.

The attempt to relieve the occupation of Budapest,
has failed. The material superiority to the enemy
is enormous.

Das Drama zwischen Budapest, Plattensee und Wien Frühling 1945.

Drama between Budapest, Lake Balaton and Vienna, Spring 1945.

Im unwegsamen Gelände ist die Versorgung nicht mehr sicher. Munition wird hinter der Hauptkampflinie vergraben und nach Bedarf abgeholt.

Supplies are no longer assured through impassable terrain. Ammunition is buried behind the front line and fetched as required.

Getarnter „Panther" in der Abwehrstellung. „Heinrich-Major" I. Abteilung Panzerregiment „Das Reich".

A camouflaged „Panther" in the defensive position. „Heinrich-Major" I Battalion Panzer Regiment „Das Reich".

Sturmgeschütze munitionieren auch aus „Rücklagen".

Assault guns too get ammunition from „caches left behind".

Der Kampfkommandant von Wien,
General Rudolf von Bünau
(Eichenlaub zum Ritterkreuz) am 13.4.45.

The commander of the fighting in Vienna,
General Rudolf von Bünau
(Knight's Cross with Oak Leaves) on 13.4.45.

General von Bünau mit seinem Ia
bei den vordersten Sicherungen —
es geht rasch dem Untergang des Reiches
entgegen.

Die letzten intakten Waffen
und der letzte Panzer IV. —
Grenadiere gehen in Stellung,
der Panzer wird Minuten später abgeschossen.

General v. Bünau with his senior staff officer
in the forward defensive positions — the
destruction of the Reich is imminent.

The remaining intact weapons
and the last Panzer IV. Grenadiers move into position.
The panzer is knocked out, a few minutes later.

Straßenkampf in Wien gegen russische Panzer.
2. SS-Panzerartillerie-Regiment.

Street fighting in Vienna against Russian tanks.
2nd SS Panzer Artillery Regiment.

Regiments-Gefechtsstand „DF" in Wien.

Regimental command post „DF" in Vienna.

Die Kameradschaft zwischen den Soldaten des Heeres und der Waffen-SS blieb bis zum Ende.

The comradeship between soldiers of the Army and the Waffen-SS continued to the end.

279

Verwundet steht an der Floridsdorfer Brücke der Divisionskommandeur, SS-Standartenführer Rudolf Lehmann, links Obersturmbannführer Weidinger, rechts Ordonnanzoffizier. Wien 13.4.45.

The divisional commander SS Standartenführer Rudolf Lehmann stands wounded on the Floridsdorf Bridge, at the left Obersturmbannführer Weidinger, at the right orderly officer. Vienna 13.4.45.

Im Vorfeld der Floridsdorfer Brücke 13.4.45 in Wien.

In the foreground, the Floridsdorf Bridge in Vienna, 13.4.45.

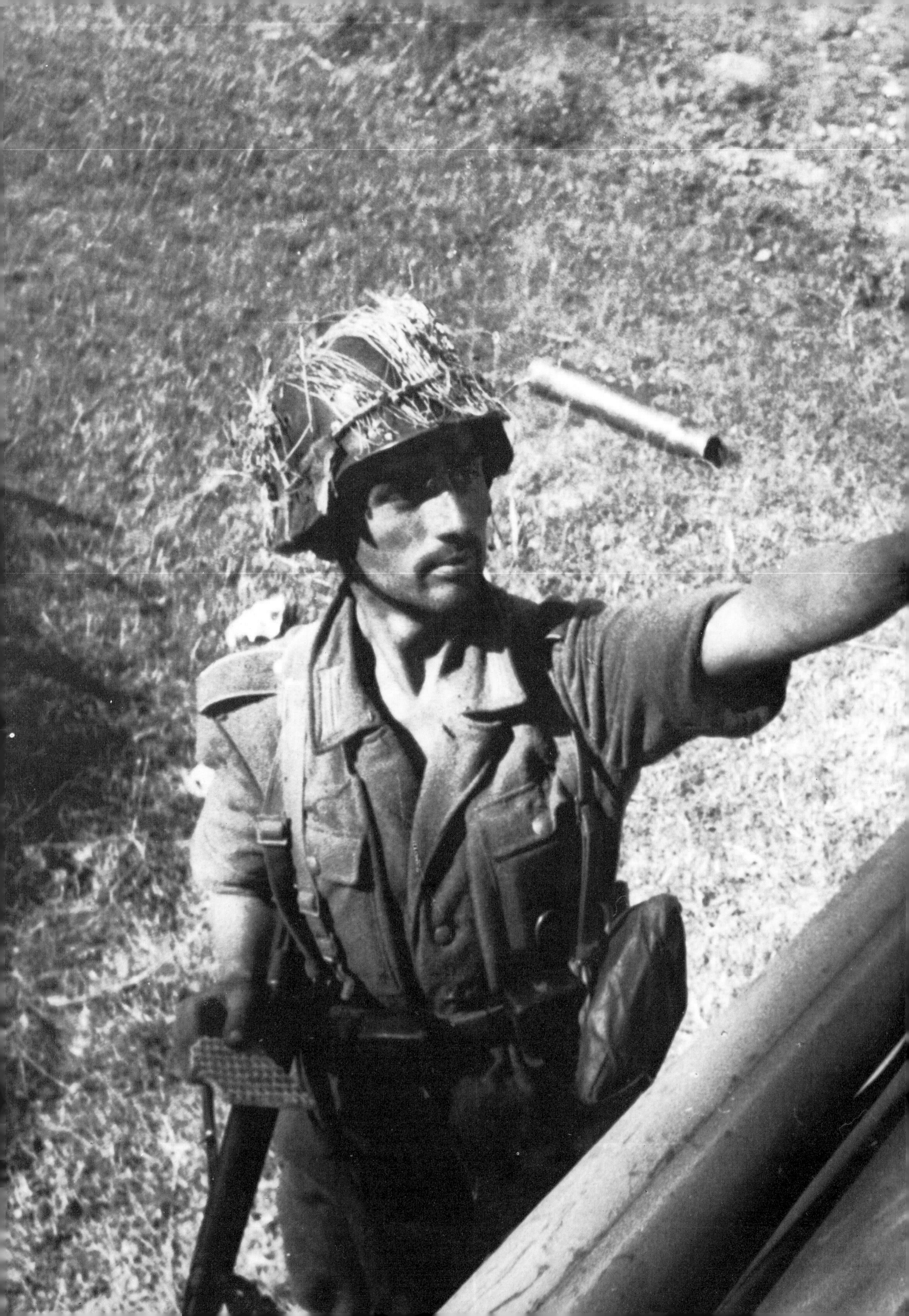

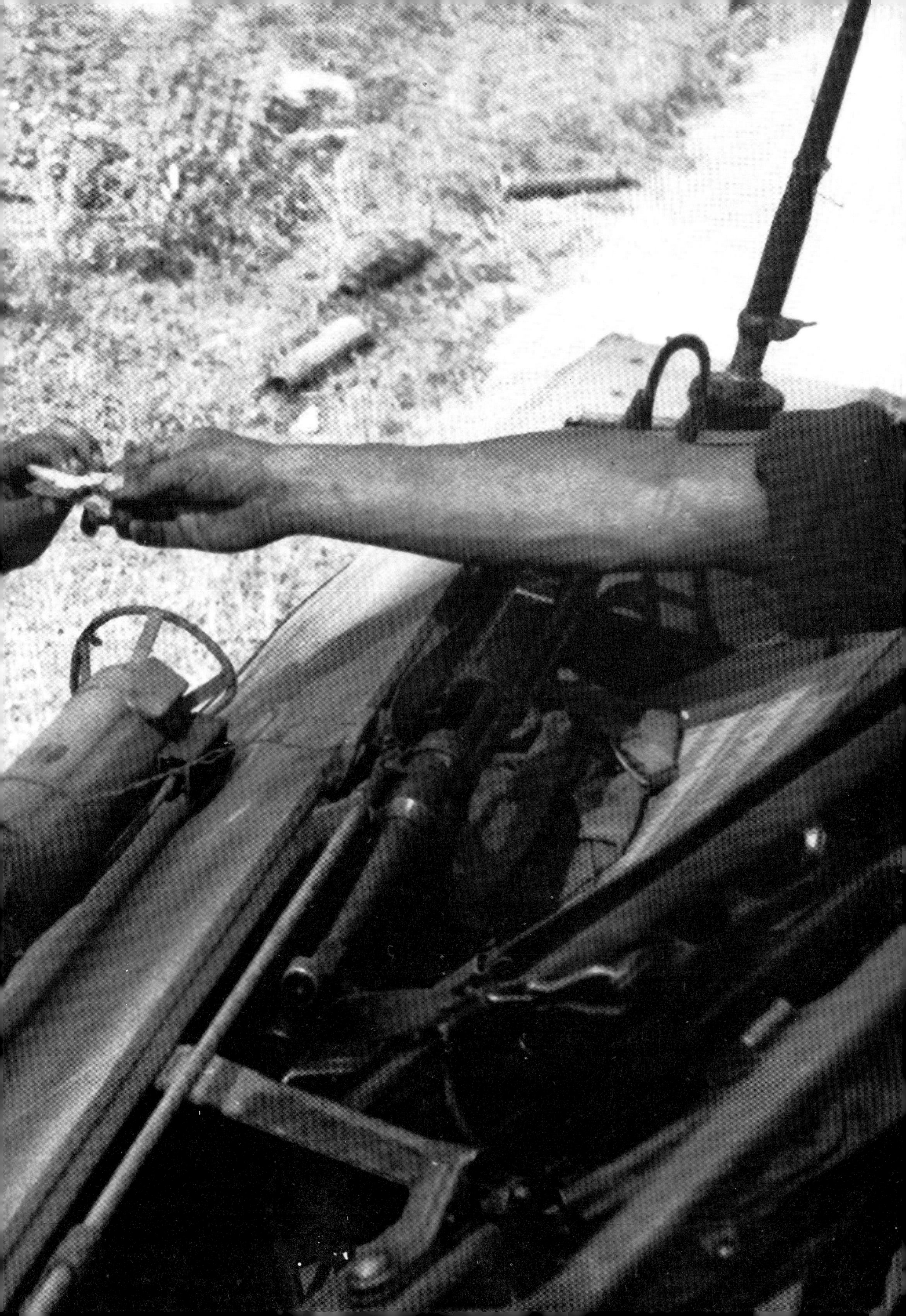

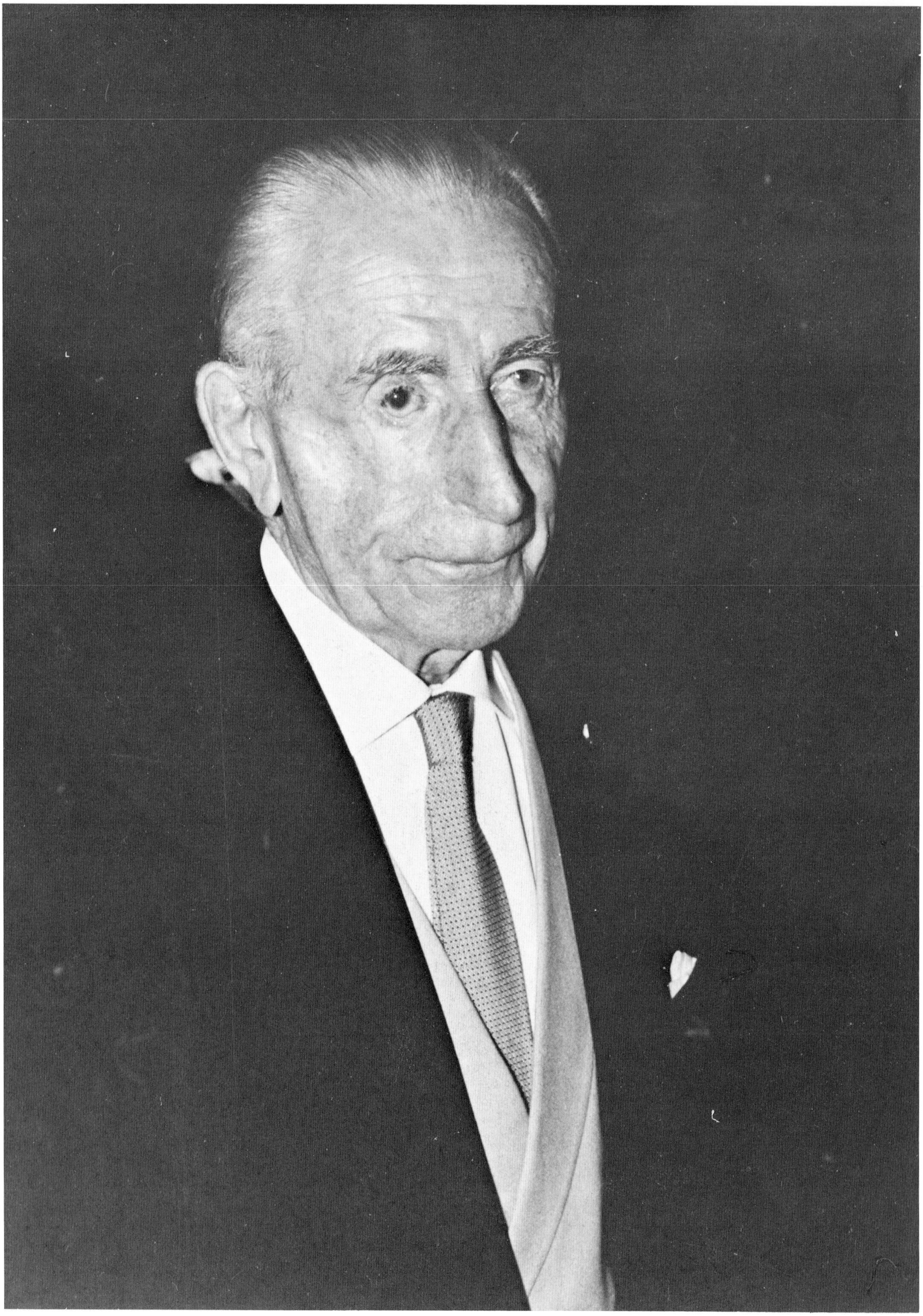

Paul Hausser
1880–1972

Ist dies nun alles miteinander das Bild des Soldaten der einstigen SS-Panzerdivision „Das Reich"?

Es war nicht die Absicht, von einzelnen zu sprechen, sie zu portraitieren und nebeneinander zu stellen. Es sollte einmal die Rede sein von Männern, die das Gewehr in die Hand nahmen oder in einen Panzer stiegen und treu, namenlos und gehorsam ihren Weg gingen.

Jeder soll sagen können: Das bin ja ich?!

Er wird es ganz leise vor sich hinsagen. Denn dort, wo gekämpft wurde und gestorben, versagt die Beredsamkeit.

In aller Bescheidenheit will dieser Bildband nur eine Erinnerung sein. Er soll später einmal sprechen zu denen, die nie den heißen Atem jener Tage verspürten. Kameradschaft braucht keinen Dank, kein Lob — zu ihrer Erneuerung braucht sie nur den Blick zurück zu den Erprobten.

Is all this together then the picture of the soldiers of the former SS Panzer Division „Das Reich"?
It was not the intention to speak of individuals, portray them, and set them up side by side, but rather to speak of men who, taking their rifles in their hands or climbing into their panzers, went on their way loyally, anonymously and obediently.
Each of them should be able to say, „That could be me!"
He will say it very softly to himself. For there where there is fighting and death, the power of words is impotent.
This book of photographs wants simply to be a modest act of remembrance. Later it should speak to those who never felt the fiery breath of those days. Comradeship needs no thanks, no praise. To renew it, all that is needed is to look back to those who have proved its worth.

Nach dem Kriege

After the war

Beim gemeinsamen Studium
der Kesselschlacht von Falaise.
Von rechts nach links:
Oberst Czarnetzki (Polen),
damals Ia 1. polnische
Panzerdivision; ein Professor
der Ecole Militaire Superior,
(Kriegsgeschichte),
Frankreich; Heinz Werner und
Otto Weidinger,
beide Panzerdivision
„Das Reich".

A communal study of the Battle
of the Falaise Pocket.
From right to left:
Colonel Czarnetzki (Poland), at the
time the senior staff officer of the 1st
Polish Division; one Professor
of the Ecole Militaire Supérior,
(war history), France; Heinz Werner
and Otto Weidinger, both of the
Panzer Division „Das Reich".

Dienstgrade der Waffen-SS, des Heeres und anglo-amerik. Streitkräfte
Equivalent Ranks in Waffen-SS, German Army and Anglo-American Forces

SS-Mann	Grenadier	No equivalent
SS-Sturmmann	Gefreiter	Private
SS-Rottenführer	Obergefreiter	Private First Class
SS-Unterscharführer	Unteroffizier	Corporal
SS-Scharführer	Unterfeldwebel	Sergeant
SS-Oberscharführer	Feldwebel	Staff Sergeant
SS-Hauptscharführer	Oberfeldwebel	Technical Sergeant
SS-Sturmscharführer	Stabsfeldwebel	Master Sergeant
SS-Untersturmführer	Leutnant	2nd Lieutenant
SS-Obersturmführer	Oberleutnant	1st Lieutenant
SS-Hauptsturmführer	Hauptmann	Captain
SS-Sturmbannführer	Major	Major
SS-Obersturmbannführer	Oberstleutnant	Lieutenant Colonel
SS-Standartenführer	Oberst	Colonel
SS-Oberführer	No equivalent	No equivalent
SS-Brigadeführer	Generalmajor	Brigadier General
SS-Gruppenführer	Generalleutnant	Major General
SS-Obergruppenführer	General der Infanterie	Lieutenant General
SS-Oberstgruppenführer	Generaloberst	General

Für die in diesem Bildband der SS-Panzerdivision DAS REICH gezeigten Fotographien hätten wir vielen Einzelnen unter Nennung ihres Namens zu danken, ist doch die Mehrzahl der Bilddokumente aus privaten Fotoalben zur Verfügung gestellt worden.

Die Sammlung und Herausgabe konnte nur gelingen, weil das notwendige Vertrauensverhältnis bestand, und es wird keine Stelle geben, die aus einer Division aus Frieden und Kriegszeit einer solchen Ausbeute fähig wäre.

Autor und Verlag danken herzlich.

For the photographs published in this book of illustrations („Bildband") we would have to thank so many indivudual persons by their names, for the majority of the documents provided to us derive from private albums.

The collection and publication could only be successful, since there was an inevitable feeling of confidence, and there will be no authority, that would be able to proceede out of one Division in peace and wartime.

Author and publishing house thank very much.

15.7.1939 – 18.1.1943

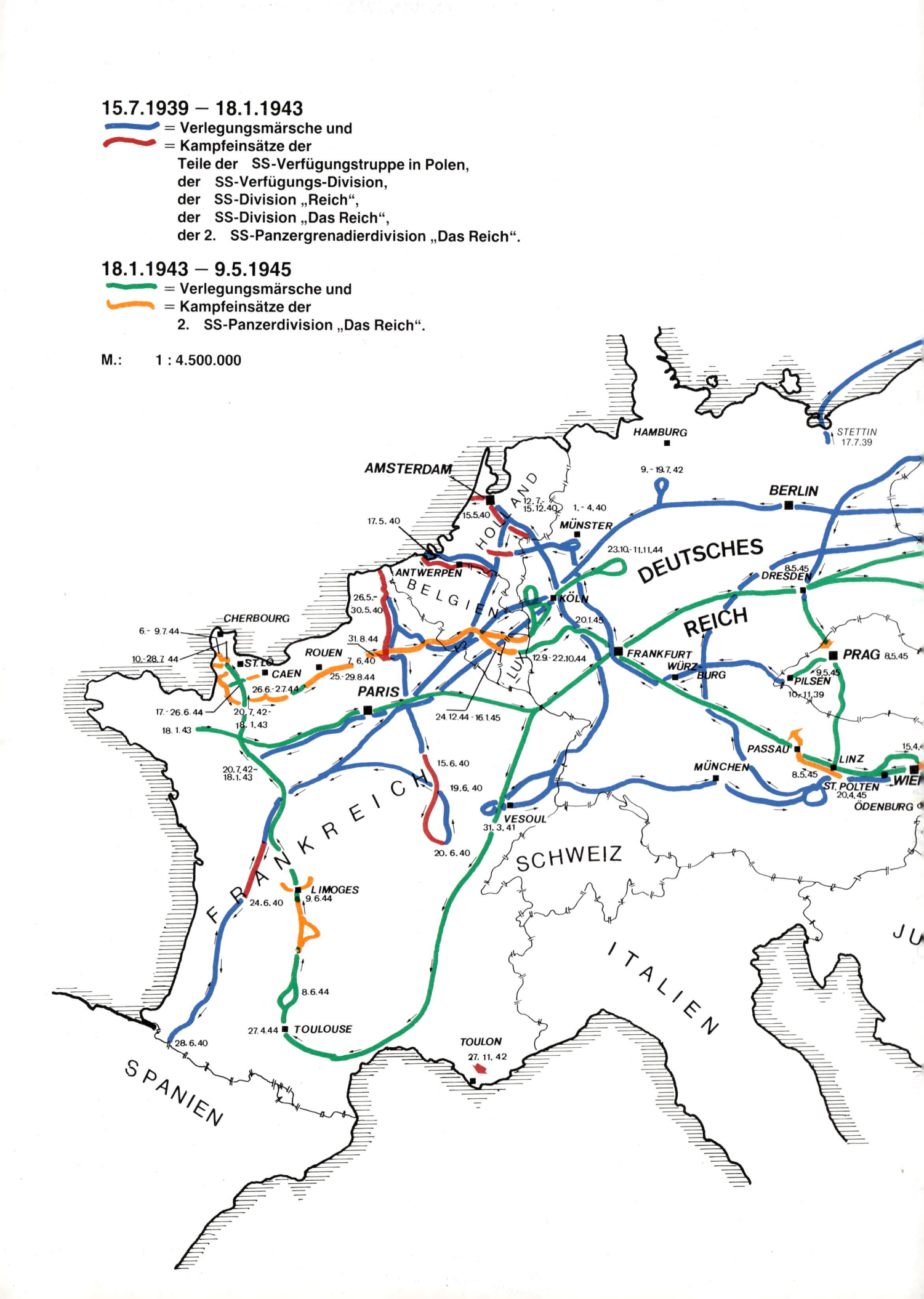

━━ = Verlegungsmärsche und
━━ = Kampfeinsätze der
  Teile der SS-Verfügungstruppe in Polen,
  der SS-Verfügungs-Division,
  der SS-Division „Reich",
  der SS-Division „Das Reich",
  der 2. SS-Panzergrenadierdivision „Das Reich".

18.1.1943 – 9.5.1945

━━ = Verlegungsmärsche und
━━ = Kampfeinsätze der
  2. SS-Panzerdivision „Das Reich".

M.: 1 : 4.500.000